THE BLOSSOM
OF A WILLOW TREE

A true story about resilience, re-birth and second chances

MARI CURTEANU

The Wisdom of a Willow Tree by Mari Curteanu

1st Edition Paperback 16th March 2022

First published in the United Kingdom

ISBN: 978-1-3999-1841-1

Book cover photography: Ercan Nurettin YILDIRIM
Cover Design and Interior Formatting: Jose Pepito Jr.
Developmental Editing: Hugh Barker
Literary Editor: Paula T. Curteanu

Printed by Lightning Source 2022

I Dedicate This Book

To my only son.

To my loving family.

To all my friends who I call family too.

To my guardian Angel Raphael and to my Creator.

Contents

PART THREE
THE LAST MOUNTAIN

INTRODUCTION

THE WILLOW TREE BY THE RIVER OF LIFE

I feel immersed in the golden sunset at the line between the earth and heavens. It's mesmerizing to witness such magnificence. My soul is melting as my eyes absorb this magical sight. It permeates every particle of my being. I'm forgetting who I am and feeling like I am almost losing myself. Who could craft such beauty?

The gentle whispers of the river are calling me back to awareness. It feels as if they're trying to reveal great secrets in a language I can't yet begin to understand. I see the sparkles of the golden sun reflected in the water, like precious diamonds at the bottom of the river. It is a river that seems to mind its own path, flowing gently but decisively towards a mysterious destination.

I close my eyes, feel the breeze on my face, and tilt it towards the sun. Its warmth kisses my skin. My soul smiles with gratitude and every cell of my body is filled with light and love for life. Warm tears of joy slide down my cheeks and I feel at one with everything around me.

I lose any sense of time. I'm not sure if I'm still in the same spot or if I have transcended it and gone to another place.

I open my eyes to reassure myself, and, by the side of the river, I see it. The willow tree. A beautiful, gracious silhouette that complements this magic sunset. Its branches are delicate and flexible. Its movements are soft and gracious, like a prima ballerina joining this mystic dance with nature. At times, the dance is soft and sweet. At other times, it is spectacular and breathtaking. It is the dance of existence, a perfect symphony of nature, like the long hair of a beautiful girl surrendering to the breeze.

I see complete surrender and openness to nature's flow. No matter how much it has to bend, the willow tree won't break, because it trusts and follows the flow of mother earth. It's a perfect picture of balance, stability and strength, flexibility and harmony, innate wisdom and resilience. The wisdom that resides within its existence, is given by Mother Nature herself. Its resilience, is the ability to embrace and rise above any challenge that comes along the way.

To me, this tree brings a powerful message.

Root yourself deeply in values and beliefs that keep you grounded and nourished. Stand tall, strong and healthy in your physical body. Have an open mind that allows you to adjust to the powerful flow of life. Trust and surrender your whole being to the grand dance of Mother Nature.

Nature has a powerful way to show us how to flow with life. If only we would be willing to appreciate it and observe its teachings. Flowers never ask for more sun and water. They just bloom in their own time. Trees don't complain about the wind and the rain, they just rise up. They can grow in the most unexpected places, like in between rocks in the most unfavourable conditions. Nature never complains, it uses the energy from the sun as it is given, and thrives despites all the adversities.

Birds are carried by the air, they don't struggle to fly by themselves. It's the air under their wings keeping them floating in the sky. Everything in nature is inextricably and intelligently interconnected.

As humans, we are called upon to witness and join this dance of nature. We need to welcome life with acceptance and flexibility. The challenge of this journey comes when we forget that we are part of nature. We are invited to embrace and receive every experience as it presents itself, and surrender to its powerful flow. When stormy days are imminent, there is nowhere to hide, so we must prepare for them, just as everything that is part of nature does.

Therefore, just as a wise sailor knows when to adjust the sails, in the course of life, we can be flexible and adjust our mind and existence to whatever comes along.

Sometimes we can't see a meaning in the moment; but later, it will all make sense. Most of the storms are there to push us further in life. They may blow and stir everything in their way, seemingly making no sense whatsoever, but when it's all done, you might find yourself in the most peaceful place you've ever imagined possible.

They say that your life is the summary of your greatest decisions and that your destiny is shaped by the choices you make in life. That is very true.

I have taken many decisions that have shaped my destiny while sailing on this river. I am going to share the stories with you in this book, and describe how I only truly learnt the wisdom of the willow tree during the year of 2019.

While it was unfolding, I thought that 2019 was the worst year of my life. However, as it turned out, it was just miracle after miracle after miracle.

Before I take you there, I would love to invite you on a short journey back to where life began for me.

PART ONE

DECISIONS SHAPE YOUR LIFE

AND THIS IS
WHERE THE STORY BEGINS

I was the first of three daughters who were given life by the love of two wonderful, simple people. They went to school together, fell in love and married very young somewhere in the countryside close to Bucharest, the capital city of Romania.

I was born when my parents were 19. They didn't pursue higher education. Instead, they wanted to have their own little family at a young age, which meant they had to earn their living from very early in life. They were travelling many hours every day to get to work in the city in order to provide for their little ones.

We were raised in a modest home and learnt to appreciate the meaningful little things, like a warm plate of food made with love after getting back from a long walk from school on a windy day. Or a new pair of winter boots, which was pretty much the only pair of shoes that would get you through the whole winter that year. Things that we take for granted nowadays.

As a first grandchild, I spent the first three years of my life being mostly raised by my grandparents on my dad's side. My first sister came just over a year after me, and she was looked after by my grandparents on my mum's side. All of this, so that my parents could continue to work in the city and provide the financial support. Back then, babysitting was a grandparent thing, clearly.

My grandparents had a beautiful home in the countryside. They grew their own fruit and vegetables and had a few farm animals. Even though

I can't recall that period in detail, I still remember being a tomboy and climbing all the trees in the backyard during the summer holidays. The taste of the fresh cherries and sour apples straight from the source is powerfully imprinted in my memory.

I can also recall the feeling of walking with my bare feet on the soft grass, the smell of my grandmother's baked bread, the taste of the fresh goat's cheese and milk my grandfather used to make from their cattle and the unique taste of the veggies from their garden.

Today they are not with us anymore, and I miss them dearly. They were just like my parents. Sometimes I feel it's maybe even more than that.

I used to love watching the blue sky for hours, lying in the field. I still love to do that, by the way. This is how you'd spent your time when you didn't have Wi-Fi and social platforms, as we do nowadays.

When I was around three or four years old, my parents found a small house and decided to move to the city with their new family. It was much easier skipping all the hours travelling and they could now afford their own place to live. Shortly after that, my sister and I had to join kindergarten.

My first memory as a child is of the four of us as a family. We were in a theme park. I remember my sister sitting next to me strapped into a carousel chair that looked like a tiny aeroplane. We were both happy and smiling. I don't even know why I have retained these details, but I can still picture her wearing a white dress with a pattern of small roses and a white hat with pink decorations. She looks just like a little princess with her curly hair. I was wearing exactly the same clothes.

This reminds me of the fact that, until we got much older, my mum used to dress us identically. Wherever we went, people thought we were twins. This happened until we were seven or eight years old when she stopped doing that. Anyhow, back to my first child memory!

It seemed like we were flying, as the carousel slowly made circles in the air. The blue sky and sunny day made everything feel like a dream. With one hand I was holding my hat, as I didn't want to lose it in the wind, and with the other hand I was waving at my parents who were watching us from the ground and waving back, smiling and blowing kisses. I love this memory. There are many warm sentiments that rise to the surface every time I replay it in my mind.

Kindergarten was the first place where I had to interact with children of my own age, other than my sister. It also involved eating foods that were not made by any of my family members. I have to confess, I struggled with this one at first. So much so, that there was a little "incident" one day at lunch time.

Back then, during the communist economy, we did not have a designated place to eat, like a canteen. Instead, they used to align all the tables in the middle of the hallway, to make one big long table, covered nicely with a tablecloth and with many chairs on both sides. It was big enough for all of us. If my mind isn't tricking me, there were at least 30 kids at that time. Thus, it was a crowded lunch table and we all sat very close to each other.

That day they served us spinach for lunch. I tried it, but could not convince myself to eat it. I did not really like spinach back then. I don't think any kid likes it at first. At the same time, I knew that I could not leave the table if I did not finish my food. That was the rule. I felt trapped for a bit, until this brilliant idea came to me. As I was taking a spoonful from the plate of spinach in front of me, instead of moving the spoon towards my mouth, I carefully looked around and when no one could see me, I rapidly threw it under the table at my feet.

I know... that was terrible. But I had to save myself and I continued the same tactic, until all the spinach was transferred from the plate to the floor. The plate was empty, so I quickly got up and ran to the bathroom to wash my hands and then rushed back to class. As I was hiding in the classroom, in my little monkey mind, I figured that, once they removed the tables from the hallway, they would see the spinach on the floor. I was worried that I might get into trouble.

Therefore, every now and then I'd stick my head out the door to check what happened out there. I could see them starting to move the chairs and then the tables away. I remember feeling very scared. After sticking my head out a few times, I looked again and there it was! Right in the middle of the hallway: my mountain of spinach.

3

Now, I can laugh out loud just picturing the whole thing in my mind, but back then, I was terrified. I hurried back in and stayed very quiet until it was all cleaned up. Nobody knew it was me. Phew! I made it.

Our little sister came when I was eight years old. I remember eating some of her baby food, when I was supposed to be feeding her instead. When she started solid food, my mum would leave me in charge of preparing her meals. The meal was grated fresh apple, soft fresh cow cheese and crushed biscuits. I had to mix it all together and feed her spoon by spoon at specific times. That was the instruction.

I can still remember the taste. It was so delicious; I would happily eat it right now. The first time I fed her went something like this: one spoon for her and two spoons for myself. Fortunately, once it occurred to me that it was delicious, I started to prepare more of it, so there would be enough for both of us.

She was so cute when she was a baby and we all loved and pampered her. She was a very peaceful, obedient child and still has these traits and much more to this day.

I remember this one time at Easter. We were visiting our grandparents, as we did every Easter holiday. For us Christians, the rising of Jesus is one of the most significant celebrations of Christianity. It's even bigger than Christmas. Every Easter we would all get up early in the morning. Then all of our family would dress up, wearing something new preferably, and we'd make our way to the church to praise Jesus.

At the end of the ceremony, every single member of the family would receive a teaspoon of the Holy Communion, which consisted of bread that had been blessed, then soaked in sacred wine. The bread represented the body of Jesus and the wine was His blood. Once everyone received the sacred gift of Jesus, we'd all walk home to prepare for the rest of the celebration, which involved a lot of cooking, eating and drinking, a tradition that is still being respected today.

As we were walking back home, I noticed that my baby sister was terribly quiet. She was holding my mum's hand as we were all walking home.

She must have been around four years old. It was unusual for her to be so quiet but I did not pay much attention.

Once we arrived home, she suddenly stopped and vigorously pulled my mum's arm with one hand; with the other, she was pointing to her mouth mumbling something. I could not hear what she said, but my mom did.

The next thing I saw, was my mum holding her palm open in front of her little mouth and my little sister spitting out something in her hand. The next instant, I figured out what it was.

All the way home, she had kept the communion in her mouth as she could not swallow it, because of the wine. What kid likes wine? At the same time, in her little mind and heart, she could not bring herself to spit it out, as deep down she understood it was sacred. She was always quite spiritual. In fact, we were all brought up like that. My poor little sister, I went and hugged her and we went away to play, so she could forget all about this experience.

We were all very close and blessed to be raised in a loving environment, despite the limitations of the socialist regime of the country back then.

At school, I was shy to begin with, but as the years went by, I was beginning to make friends and to naturally blend in with other kids in my class. A couple of them were my next-door neighbours. It was cool that they lived in the same block. That meant we would always walk together back home, having each other's back while talking all sort of cute childish nonsense on the way home.

As a teenager, I was very energetic, getting involved in all kind of extracurricular activities, mostly sports-related. I remember how I'd leave the house in the morning, rushing out the door with a piece of toast in my mouth while pulling my jacket on, and returning at suppertime, exhausted but so happy.

From the moment I stepped in, I would be able to smell the supper my mum cooked. She would always wait for me with warm food on the table and the first thing she would say when she saw me walking in was, "Finally you are home; what did you eat all day?"

At school, I was number one at the long jump and 100 meters sprint.

I was also good at foreign languages and mathematics. My father was very proud of the fact that I could untangle second grade maths calculations, while other children at school were still learning to write the numbers.

What's rewarded is reinforced, and my father's encouragement for my brilliance pumped me up for a while. But, despite all the validation, my love for maths did not last for long. A few years later I fell in love with martial arts and dancing instead. I had a teenage temperament, I guess.

One day, around the early years of my adolescence, I remember my mom and my grandmother barging through the door and announcing: "We saw people covered in blood and shooting in the middle of the street!" After that revolution, the country was freed from the communist leadership and everything started to change ever since.

When I was around 14, I started to take regular dancing classes at the junior National Theatre ballet team in Bucharest. That consumed most of my teenager energy of which I had plenty. It was perfect for me. I loved those years. It seemed that I was good at it and, before you know it, I was part of a group led by a great choreographer that was putting on shows all over the country. These were performances that could take part anywhere in Romania, which meant I could travel around and was even being paid for it.

I would be rehearsing for these performances most of the time after school. Between 15 and 17 years of age, there were always some sorts of events and shows going on. I recall spending whole summers at the best seaside resorts in Romania, sharing the stage with famous artists of the time, some of whom are still well known to this day. It was cool to spend summers there and making some pocket money as well.

My parents were supportive and they trusted me, which meant I had a lot of freedom. They were also happy that I could take care of myself throughout those summers without needing their support.

During my free time after school, at least when in the off-season, I used to love spending time with friends. We were a big bunch. I remember this café in the centre of Bucharest, where they use to make the most amazing cakes. I used to spend all my pocket money taking them there and offering to buy them cakes.

When the money was finished, I used to "borrow" some more from my mom's purse, just to get to do that again the day after. We used to sit and chat until we lost track of time. There were no digital connections at that time, just real connections. They were great times.

I remember one day, this gypsy woman came by our table and grabbed my hand to read my palm. I pulled it back and said, "I don't have any change for you". In fact, I only had a bill of 10 Lei, which at the time was a lot of money for a teenager. She insisted and said "I won't touch your money, let me do it". We all felt a bit intimidated by her, but I allowed her to go ahead quickly so that she can leave us in peace.

She took my hand again and said: "You will travel to far away lands, over big waters and mountains, and everywhere you will go, I see people looking up to you with big eyes." She said other things as well, but these are the only words that stayed with me. I had no clue what she meant back then, but later in life, it all clicked. The funny part is that in the end, she tricked me. She continued: "Now place the bill on your palm, I will not steal it, don't worry". I believed her and did as she said. Then, she slightly leaned over and spat on the bill for "good luck". "Ewww!", I exclaimed. And that is how I literally threw my money on her.

Before I knew it, I was 18 and the high school years had come to an end. I was at that point in life, where I had to decide in which direction my journey and further education would continue.

However, before I could do that, something incredible happened.

MARRY YOUNG AND RUN AWAY

S ociety is prone to setting a sequence of benchmarks when it comes to achieving the "targets and accomplishments of life".

For instance, it teaches us to study hard and get good grades at school. Then study some more, get a good degree, professional qualification, a job that pays well, build up a career, get married and have kids by your 30s, pay your taxes, and hopefully live happily ever after until you die.

This is the sequence that is supposed to make you feel fulfilled and that you have achieved your targets in life, right? Well, not quite... at least not for me.

Most people don't have kids by their 30s and sometimes don't even have a job and that's OK. Everyone gets to walk their own path in their own time and that's for each individual to decide what it should be. Not everyone has to fit in with the picture-perfect society frame, nor do they have to follow any particular way of living their life.

I haven't followed that sequence at all. In fact, I started "upside down". I believe it's not the particular sequence of the decisions, but the timing and place from which we take those decisions, that shape our lives.

Life is a pattern that often repeats itself, and of course, just as my parents had done, I fell in love and married young, right after high school. Any thoughts of further education were gone with the wind.

9

Long story short, I met this man, a Greek Cypriot, who fell in love with me. He didn't think I was Romanian. It felt charming when he said that my beautiful darker shades made me look like a more exotic creature, something that "he'd never seen before". My English was very good as it was pretty much the only subject in which I was still excelling at in school. We just kind of clicked. The attraction was mutual; at least that's what I thought at the time. He was twelve years older than me, and I was just a baby, if you know what I mean. I think my brain was still developing in that respect, and to be honest, I did not have much experience with men at that time.

When the time came for him to leave, he convinced me that he was in love with me. He said he just could not go back without me. He bought me a ticket to fly with him, at least for a holiday. I was thrilled. We caught the plane, and landed in Cyprus but I could not cross the border, as there was some problem with my visa. I was simply not allowed to enter the country, so I had to fly back to Bucharest that same evening.

He just bought another ticket and flew back with me a few hours later, on the same plane. That was incredibly romantic, so you can imagine that I was instantly hooked. I still remember my parents' faces when they saw us back home.

He figured that the only way to make me his was to marry me and take me away for good. I didn't resist this; on the contrary, I agreed to all of it. I guess a part of me wanted the cavalier in his shiny armour to fight for me.

My parents did not really approve, as it was all happening so fast. I was suddenly in a relationship, and then a marriage, and they were definitely not ready to "lose" me yet. However, after a long talk and list of warnings, they did give me their blessing.

We got married, I changed my passport to have matching names, and I was looking forward to this new chapter of my life.

My heart was sore about having to leave behind my sisters and parents, my home, my friends and all that I knew. At the same time, the excitement of a new beginning with someone I loved and the idea of living in a sunny place and a beach was all enchanting. That added a bit of honey to my bitter drink. And just like that, a couple of weeks later, I moved to sunny Cyprus with my new Greek Cypriot husband, who was also the first man in my life.

Yes… I was one of those old schoolgirls who saved herself for marriage. Now, later in life, I ask myself, "Where was my brain?" I doubt I even had one at the time. Never mind, I guess it was all meant to be.

I fell in love with the climate, the sea, and the calm and laid-back vibe of the island, which was nothing like the city back home. Everything was new and it all seemed so abundant. I loved the shops and the vibrant colours: the shoes, the dresses and all the sparkle a girl of 18 would be drawn to. He would buy me all the things I wanted and I am not going to lie, I enjoyed all of it. But this did not last for long.

As the months passed following this radical change of environment, it didn't take long before I realised that my decision was beginning to cause me a great deal of emotional pain. How did I ever think that it was going to be easy, moving away to a place where I knew nobody, did not speak the language and had absolutely no friends or anywhere to go? In addition, I had the painful realisation that my husband was now entirely emotionally absent from our relationship.

But it was too late; I got pregnant straight away and was too proud to go back to my parents and tell them that they had been right about everything. I was missing my family and friends a great deal and began to feel very lonely and sad over time.

I remember one evening around a month before Christmas, I was all alone, pregnant and crying all night while watching the flickering lights of the Christmas tree. I couldn't keep the tears back as I tried to figure out how I had found myself in that situation. I had left a place that was home, with family and friends and a fun and happy life, to move to this new place. A beautiful paradise it might have been, but I knew nobody, didn't speak the language and had no friends at all.

What was I thinking, when I took that big decision to fly away with a man I barely even knew? Clearly, I was in way over my head and had no idea what I was doing. I felt like he had lied and hadn't been honest about his feelings. But then, why would he go to the extent of getting married if he did not love me? I was doubting everything, but mostly myself. I had really thought that he would never break my heart when I decided to say yes. But that is not the only reason why people should get married, right? However, at that time, I had no idea what a romantic relationship was about, because I had never really had one. All I knew in my heart was that I loved him and it was painful.

Most of the day, he was nowhere to be found. He would only come in to eat and change his clothes, then he would go out "working" again. He would do all the right things but he could not hold space for me when it came to emotional connection.

Sometimes he would take me for a ride or drop me at his mum's and leave me there for hours, where I'd have to pretend that everything was fine. His family were all lovely people, but I could not really communicate much with his parents, as they only spoke Greek and all I could speak at the time was English and Romanian.

When you are expecting a child, it's supposed to be a wonderful time in your life where you bond both with the baby to be born, and also with your other half. This was not the case for me. Whenever I tried to talk to him and work out what was going on, he would become furious and we would end up having huge fights and arguments, which would make me feel even worse than before. I was pregnant and didn't need to be dealing with that kind of emotional distress.

It was the lowest I'd ever felt in my life to that point. I could not get myself to tell my family the truth about what was going on, so I decided to suffer in silence. I wasn't strong enough to take any action. Well, at least, not at that time.

STICK TO IT AND MAKE IT RIGHT

I was feeling deeply guilty for the nightmare I was living, as I realised how I had rushed into this decision. I felt that it was all my fault and there was no way I could undo it. I held myself responsible for my own pain and struggle, because of the poor judgement I had shown. I understood that I had been blinded by the desire for freedom and adventure. I had thought that the grass would be greener on the other side, but I had been wrong. However, when I was done beating myself up, I decided to take full responsibility for my own actions.

I guess there was an essential part of me that drove me to this choice. Decisions are always driven from within, by something deeply wired inside yourself. Most of the time we don't even know it's there. However, it still drives our actions. That was the part that wanted me to be responsible. I'd learnt a sense of responsibility since I was a little girl. My parents were busy working hard and providing for their new family. I was the older sister, the one that had to be responsible for her two little sisters while they were away. I guess, that is where my sense of accountability came from, and now I really needed it.

Before I could make that switch though, I felt trapped, weak and powerless for a long time. The young woman in me was wounded. One day, as I was drowning in floods of tears and I was beating myself up with miserable thoughts and sad emotions, I felt my little baby kicking inside my tummy.

In that instant, all the negative thoughts I had, just vanished. I immediately stopped living in my head and returned to my body. It was as though someone wanted to send me a reminder of a better future. In that moment I realised that I would have never had this baby, if all this hadn't happened. For some strange reason, I felt like it was worth the sacrifice. I felt like the universe wanted me to wipe my tears and see the miracle of being blessed with a child. And so, I did.

A fresh breeze of recharged energy magically came over me. I was instantly called to direct all my attention and passion for life into something new. I had a desire to learn after that.

I knew I could not change anything about my husband; I could only change myself and the way I saw things. This decision left me with one option: to do my best with what I had.

I somehow managed to work through that numb pain and to shift my focus onto myself and my baby. I decided to read more and discover new things. Soon afterwards, I started to learn the local language. Greek isn't an easy language, but I knew it couldn't be impossible. I had all the time in the world, so I bought myself some dictionaries and watched a great deal of English movies with Greek subtitles. That helped; it was entertaining and it seemed easy. It kept me busy as well.

At the same time, I was reading loads about the pre and post-pregnancy phases. I felt the need to know more about my soon to be born baby. I bought myself a few books and started reading them cover to cover. It was great to be focusing my energy on something useful. I began dreaming about how my life would change when I became a mother. I had a strong connection with my unborn baby. So much so, that, even though the gynaecologist didn't reveal the gender beforehand, I always knew it was going to be a boy. And he was!

When he arrived, his skin was a light lilac colour; he had probably been struggling for air to get out faster. I will never forget the moment they've put him on my chest and I saw his beautiful big eyes looking straight into mine for the first time. I will never forget that look. They say, *a son is a mother's last true love.* Very true. My maternal instinct ignited and we bonded for life. I remember spending all my time in the nursery the few days after he was born. All the staff and nurses working at the clinic were encouraging me to go and rest in my own room, but I just could not be away from him. Once you have a baby, everything shifts, and your own life comes second. If you are blessed with children, you know exactly what I am talking about.

I remember the day we left the clinic, the three of us, it was such a beautifully strange feeling. I even remember his father saying, "From now on, the baby comes first".

However, I'm not sure exactly what he meant, because over time he didn't behave that way at all. Of course, he loved his son and he showed it by spoiling him with all the clothes and toys any father would. But I noticed that, emotionally, he did not seem to be fully there. I don't think he knew how, and it probably wasn't even his fault. He did the best he knew at the time, which was to provide everything for all of us. We always had all the necessities and we even seemed like a happy family when we were going out for a ride or to a family gathering like a wedding or a christening.

However, in reality, it still felt like he wasn't really there. It was all rushed, almost as if he just wanted to get it done, so that he could go out and live his other parallel life.

He was also very jealous and he wouldn't allow me to work even when our son got older. He would provide everything for me, but partly just to make sure that I'd stay at home. Whatever I wanted, however costly, it would not be a problem.

BREAK FREE

F ast forward a few years and my marriage had become a never-ending emotional rollercoaster with regular fights and arguments. I had thought that after a while, I would be able to convince myself to see things differently, maybe in a way that could make my life easier, but it was all in vain.

He wouldn't change any of his habits. I had hoped he would be willing to stay around more, at least for his son. That was not the case. He did change for a bit. But later it only got worse. He began to be violent as well. The most painful part was that my son witnessed this most of the time, even if he was pretending that he was playing in his room.

It happened so many times that I lost count. However, I remember this one particular incident when I understood something that I hadn't before. My son was sleeping, or at least I hope he was. It was quite late. He must have been three or four years old at the time. We got into a huge fight, yet again. This time, it escalated to another level of violence. He pulled my hair so hard that I had bumps on my head afterward.

I remember trying to get myself into a corner so that I could get a break away from him; I started crying in silence, as I did not want my son to wake up. When he left the room, I took a breath of relief. A few minutes later, he came back with an ice pack he had made with a kitchen towel and a few ice cubes. He approached me again, but this time he just sat close to me. I was trembling and my soul was broken, while my face was covered in tears.

He pressed the icepack to my head. Then he started crying and mumbling something and apologising for what had just happened. He said that he did not know what had come over him, that he hadn't meant for any of this to happen, and that he loved me.

In that instant, I had an epiphany. The one who really needed help was him, not me. Even though during those moments, I was trying to keep myself from drowning in a deep sea of bitter pain, a part of me felt deeply sorry for him.

I later found out that he was using; as a result, he was addicted and anxious. This changed my perspective on things in many ways. Something had shifted in me, even though I still struggled with it. I never demanded that he stop using, as I knew it was hopeless. He was clearly struggling with his own mental and emotional issues. I felt so alone in this whole thing. The man who I had thought would never hurt me, was tearing me apart. I felt dead inside, and I knew that one day, I had to find the strength and the means to get out of that nightmare.

It felt like I was in the middle of dreadful weather with pouring rain and rough winds, and a part of me knew that it was going to get even tougher before it will get better. I could see a big storm ahead of me. My wounded heart was dripping pain. There were moments when I just wanted to break down and let it all fall on me. But there was more to this than just my own life. I couldn't give up.

My son was the one who kept me fighting to find a way out. I had to keep myself together. I knew that the only way out of it, was through it. There was a time when I thought my life was over. Towards the end, I remember there were moments when I just did not want to wake up the next day. But my son was the source of my power.

I don't know who I would have become if it wasn't for him. All I wished for, was peace of heart and mind, and a harmonious home with my son. I was scared to leave my abusive husband and worried for our safety.

By this time, both our families knew that he was violent and they were very much aware of what I was going through every day. My parents wanted me to go back, but I could not do that. He would never allow his son to be taken away from him. He threatened me that if I'd try anything, he will do everything in his power to take my son away from me and throw me out of the country.

It was really difficult and I struggled every single day for years. However, through all the pain, I've learnt that life has a magic way of restoring balance. When you don't have the power to walk away from something that is harmful, unhealthy or detrimental to your own life, it creates circumstances. I like to think of these like exits on a highway, which you can use to "escape" and readjust the course of your journey.

These are significant times when you learn that you are stronger than you'd ever imagined. The good news is that you can rise above it. The bad news, is that this happens in a very intense and painful way, which shakes you to the very core.

The day that I have found the power to walk away from this nightmare and take this exit, was the day when he attacked me in my car, when I just wanted to take my son and my middle sister for a ride. That was of course, after they had to witness him screaming around the house again. By this time, he would only come home once or twice a week, just to bring his clothes for washing. He was doing his own laundry, I was not even touching it anymore.

At that time, my middle sister was visiting, as she knew I was going through difficult times. I remember feeling so ashamed that she had to witness all of that horror. That day, she was sitting in the back seat of the car comforting her nephew.

I'd started driving and was slowly getting away from the house. At some point, I had to stop at the traffic lights. All the while, he had been furious, and driving behind us, but I hadn't noticed that.

At least, I didn't until I had to stop at that red light. That's when he jumped out of his car in the middle of traffic, and showed up by my window yelling at me to open the car door. Of course, I was petrified, so I didn't. He then squeezed his fingers through the glass, which was slightly open, and violently pulled it out. I was in shock. The whole thing shattered into pieces and some of the thick bits of glass hit my face.

All this happened with my son in the back seat. He was just six years old at the time. I can't even begin to imagine the trauma that this may have caused him, and my sister as well. She was hysterically screaming at him to stop while my son was crying in the back seat.

When we managed to get away from him, I ended up holding my son, who was crying, in despair. I realised that the one human being in the world that I'd give my life for, my own son, was in danger because of his own father. Not a stranger, but his father. This was not because he would intentionally want to harm him – he would have never done that – but because he wasn't willing to control his behaviour and temper around him. How can you undo all that psychological trauma that you cause to your own child? I hated him for that.

In that moment my animal instinct erupted. Every bit of my energy shifted. The biggest part of me became a different person. I only had one thought. *I will never let this happen again. I'm putting an end to this now.*

That is how I stepped into the most scary and uncomfortable zone of my entire life up to that point. Feeling tormented and scared after the nightmare we had been through, I somehow found the strength to drop my sister and son back home and drive to the nearest police station.

I had broken glass on my neck and clothes. I was literally shaking. I told them everything. One of the officers in charge knew him by name. They told me that they would go find him, arrest him, and keep him overnight. When I heard that, I began to shake even more, as I knew what could happen when he got out. I was terrified.

The fear of being threatened and abused at any time was very real, but the natural instinct of protecting the safety of my son and change our future, fuelled my strength. He came back in the morning after he was released, yelling my name and banging on the windows and doors. I was scared but I didn't open the door. This time, he was holding his natural aggression down, but he clearly hadn't liked being kept overnight. My door remained shut. That was the limit.

And that is how the magic universe works to restore harmony, even when you don't know where to begin. Yes, there may be a great amount of pain involved, but it is also the fastest route out in these situations.

There was no way back after that, and the divorce papers followed soon after. I knew it was going to be hard until he got used to the idea. And he did eventually, but only after a few years.

Before that happened, it wasn't easy for him. He had a dominating, loud personality and had a false pride with that as well. Even though he was involved in other personal relationships, he was still following me around, sometimes trying to intimidate me. All the while under the false pretence that he was doing it all in his son's best interests.

My family was still insisting I should go back home, so they could support me. It was truly hard for them to be far from me, especially when they knew how things were in my life at the time.

However, while I considered it in detail, I felt that it would be extremely hard for my son to go through such a massive change as moving countries. He was already seven years old at the time, speaking the language, making friends at school and that was his home. I knew that his parents' separation was already hard enough on him. By that time, it had been two years since I had my citizenship, which meant I also had the option to just continue to live there and build a life for the two of us. I decided to stay. It felt much easier that way and I had more opportunities there.

After many arguments and resistance, his father eventually agreed on times where he could see his son regularly. The one good thing I have to admit is that he never touched him in an abusive way. However, not all wounds are visible, and all the mental abuse that he had already caused was just as harmful in its own way. I kept in touch with him and stayed civilised for the sake of our child.

I never tried to turn my son against his dad or refused to let him go for a visit, even though deep down I was worrying every time he spent the night over at his place. At the depth of their hearts, children will always have love for their parents no matter how bad it gets. I knew my son loved his dad, I respected that and was supportive of all his wishes in that aspect.

So much so, that a few years later, his dad wanted us to be more than friends again. That was a shock. I just laughed: my answer was "Really? Are you high or something? I'm just going to pretend that I didn't even hear you say that." Fortunately, he laughed back and that was that.

Who would have thought that after all that turmoil, a day would come when he would actually sing my praises to everyone? His girlfriend would call me and tell me how highly he spoke of me and how he was telling everyone that "He took his hat off to me". His friends would tell me how he would shout out that "His ex-wife was the best". Funny life, isn't it?!

After the separation, I was very lucky to have my family's support. My parents took turns and visited me for a few months, to look after their grandson while he was at home during summer holidays and I was working. It was great to have them around, it made things so much easier for me and I needed all the help I could get.

During this transition time, I remember feeling as low as anyone would after a failed and terrifying marriage, but my vision of a beautiful and independent life with my son kept me going.

At night, I would close my eyes and dream of being free, independent, financially secure, happy. But in the meantime, the struggle was real.

A NEW START BELOW THE ZERO LINE

I n the very beginning after the divorce, I was physically, mentally and emotionally at zero. I had no professional qualifications, not to mention an empty bank account. In fact, at every level I was below zero.

Where do you start when you feel like that and you have a child to raise as well? Not an easy task, I can assure you. I was 26 at the time and my son was seven years old. Up to that point, I had never had a real job. My ex-husband had never allowed me to have a life other than that of a housewife.

The time arrived when life turned very real and I actually needed a job. At that point, I was ready to do just about anything as long as I could earn some money. I didn't mind what the job might be. I was willing to scrub floors if I had to. I was thirsty to be independent, and I felt that, as long as I was honest and kept my head high, everything would work out somehow.

For the first two years or so after the separation, I was working two jobs. In the mornings, I'd drop my son at school and then go to work in a café where I'd make sandwiches and coffee for people working in the offices. By lunchtime I'd be done and would rush to pick him up from school.

We would then go home, where we'd have lunch together. Then, in the afternoon, I was working in a rental shop for DVDs, which were in high demand at the time. I took him along with me. That worked out well for both, as he was doing his homework while he was there. He was growing more and more every day. Before I knew it, he was almost ten.

Sometimes I feel like we grew up together. I remember how he would come into my room and jump on my bed just after I had made it, to tease me. In the end, we'd both end up holding hands and jumping on my bed. Of course, that was always followed by a pillow fight.

I was a young mother with no experience of life, so I tried to raise him the best way I knew at the time. Sometimes, especially in single parent cases, we tend to want to make up for the missing half and we may end up spoiling them a bit more than necessary. I've always tried not to do that.

I recall one time when he wanted a tape for his video game. Yes, this was the beginning of the Mario/Nintendo generation. He already had many, but like every child, he wanted a new one.

Whenever he asked me for something like that, I would never say "No" or "Yes" straight away. Instead, I would say, "Let me think about it", and he would be OK with that answer for a bit. After a while, he would lose his patience, and ask me again with a slightly more persistent voice, perhaps even literally pulling my sleeve. This time I would answer, softly but firmly, "Please don't push this, do you want me to say no? I can do that straight away, but let me consider it first." And, of course, he would then say, "No, no, please think about it".

I wanted him to understand the difference between something that was necessary and something that he just wanted. He was a good kid and he understood that as a single mother, financial matters were not always easy for me. I was providing everything that he needed, but I always taught him that, even if you have all the money in the world, you should still consider this distinction.

Having said that, it's never a great thing to develop scarcity beliefs around money especially as a child, as it can have an adverse effect on your abundance mindset as you grow up. But of course, many of us have been through it, for various reasons.

I was always grateful that he never gave me any troubles. At school his teachers were singing his praises. He would come back from school and always do his homework without me having to chase him for it. He was very responsible even though he was still little. I guess that could be something I passed onto him at a cellular level.

At the time, I was reading self-help books on child psychology and how to raise children. It was always with the intention of being a good mother and maybe even helping him to overcome some of the traumatic experiences he had during his first seven years of life. It's such a hard thing to undo, but I was hopeful. Everything I read and applied was certainly very useful and helped me a lot in that respect.

I remember, we created this cool thing we both agreed to do. It was called our "break a rule thing". This one was not in the books, but I made it up myself, to make the little things more fun. We both liked the rain, for some reason. I remember having watched the rain from my window for hours, while I was pregnant with him. Maybe that was the root of it.

When it was raining heavily, instead of wrapping up and eating soup or drinking tea at home, we would jump in the car and go to buy ice cream from the drive-through at McDonalds. This was our break a rule thing and we both enjoyed it. Well... I certainly did. Those McFlurries were our favourites at that time. There is also something about the combination of driving with raindrops drumming on your windshield and the taste of ice cream that goes well together.

Our life was peaceful, and we both started to get used to the calm. The fights and screams began to fade from my memory; it started to feel like something that was long gone. Both peace and confidence were slowly starting to settle back into our lives. My son was visiting his dad regularly and he seemed to be fine with that most of the time.

However, one day, after picking him up from his dad's, where he had stayed over the weekend, he seemed a bit off as we were driving back home. He didn't have his usual energy. At that time, his dad had just divorced the woman he had married after our separation, making her his second ex-wife, and my son had met his dad's new partner that weekend.

I knew that it was a huge change for him because he had been getting along well with the one before. So, I asked him what he thought of this "new wife": "Did you like her, was she nice?"

"I preferred the one before as she was friendlier and nicer to me. This one is a bit… different," he said.

When grown-ups break up, we don't register that the ones that really take the fall are our children. We are old enough to know what we're dealing with, we have been working through the grief a long time before it happens, and yes, we get hurt but we get over it and then we move on. Kids get caught in the middle. They have to split themselves up, and deal with the break-up even more than we do. Sometimes they may even have to pretend to be someone they are not when they are jumping between the two parents.

It was sad to hear him say that, and I could sense his disappointment. I paused for a few moments, trying to think how to say something that would comfort him. He was always a bit moody after he came back from visiting his dad, but it would usually only last for a short while. As soon as he felt the comfort of being around me, everything was back to normal.

This time it was different. He was losing his sense of safety on the other side and I could not control or change that. After a minute, I felt ready and replied to him.

"I know you prefer the previous one and that you became friends because she was nice. I really liked her too. I understand that you may not like your dad's new partner much. But do you know something? We don't have to love her and we don't even have to like her that much either. We can only accept that she is your dad's wife now and respect his choice and decision."

As soon as I said that, his face lit up in a matter of seconds and he said, "Yes mama, you are right" and he leaned over to the driver's seat to hug me.

And just like that, as the years passed by, it seemed as if our boat began to float on the river and the storm was long behind us. We had everything that was necessary to experience a decent life. I had a job, we had a home, food, clothes, a car and all that was needed to feel safe. It felt good to acknowledge that.

We were also blessed to have met many wonderful people and to have a life filled with amazing friends. These people became like family over time. We would spend holidays together and there was never a Christmas without them around. It was such a beautiful feeling to have that kind of family by our side. They'd always wanted me to know that they were there for me, if I ever needed anything. And they were, each in their own perfect way.

I felt so grateful for everything I had in my life, and even though I had achieved a great deal up to that point, I woke up one day feeling that we both deserved even better. I felt like I could do better myself, as there was so much more potential in me.

I guess it felt like I just had to move to my next destination down the river. I remember thinking this way:

"I can do more than this. I want to have a job that would offer me more security and a better life for my son and myself. I want to work on something that is more complex that will help me grow and learn more, then build a career out of it. I know I have the brains for it."

Something shifted in me at that moment. It was like all my energy changed. A new current of life was flowing through me. In my mind's eye, I could see this future version of me wearing a skirt business suit and high heels, walking down the corridors and entering my own office. I not only could picture it, but I could also almost feel the taste of it. I knew that I had to meet that potential in me. What I was doing at the time suddenly seemed too easy.

I had no idea exactly how I was going to get there, but something in my gut felt right. I just knew there was something bigger and better ahead for us.

With that in mind, I had to pick myself up and take some serious action. Job-hunting with no CV and no experience? Go figure! It wasn't that easy. I didn't even know where to start, but that's when good friends and referrals come in handy. Nothing in our lives is random.

The universe is so magical. It brings everything to us, as long as we are clear on what we want and it is heartfelt. I believe that everything and everyone we know, has a role to play in our lives. God sends help and guidance through other people, who are there to support you at a given time, exactly at the moment when you are in need.

Very soon after, I was offered a position as a junior accountant in a small firm through a friend's referral, for a reasonable remuneration. I had no idea about accounting at the time, but it turned out I could easily perform bank reconciliations without too much supervision. The senior accountant showed me the steps of the process once, and it was enough. I picked it up very quickly; I was eager and thirsty to learn.

Good news travel fast and one day the director and CEO of the company called me into his office. He started by telling me that he had been impressed with my performance. Then he offered to finance my studies, if I was interested to take this further and obtain an official accounting qualification. Of course, I accepted his offer on the spot.

That's how I came to begin studying and my journey in the financial world. I remembered my dad's pride in my intelligence when I was little. I think that's where this decision came from. It comes from another deeply rooted value. I knew I was capable of it, and that I had it in me.

I started small, with the LCCI (London Chamber of Commerce and Industry qualification). I successfully passed all three levels with distinction. It was a basic certification, quite common for someone who was looking to be a bookkeeper and work in an accounting position like the one I was holding at the time.

At the office, the big boss was happy with my achievements and entrusted me with more job responsibilities. He even gave me full accountability to supervise a small portfolio of clients on a daily basis. My salary was increasing too, which was awesome.

I was always very grateful and frequently expressed my gratitude for his help. I remember after I passed all my exams and went to thank him for everything, he said:

"There is no need to thank me. This was your decision and choice. You could have said 'I'm a single mother, I have too much on my plate and I can't do this'. But you chose to go ahead despite of all the obstacles. I just did the easy part. Besides, I could always see you had the potential of a Ferrari engine even if it was hidden in a Fiat car."

I will always be grateful to this man. He believed in me, and that meant a great deal. I gained incredible experience from working there for a few years and it truly shifted the direction of my life.

CLIMBING UP
THE LADDER

I t is such a blessing to be surrounded by the right people at the right
time – friends who want to see you progress and move forward in life.
I was blessed with many souls just like that, who encouraged me along
the way. That helped me to move forward, even at times when I wasn't
feeling confident enough to believe in myself.

After getting a taste of my first professional certification and feeling
successful, I remember talking to a dear friend – I call her my soul sister –
about taking my studies even further. I had heard about a qualification
that back then was, and still is, one of the top ones in the accountancy
industry: ACCA, which stands for Association of Chartered and Certified
Accountants.

At the time I could not see myself doing that. It seemed like a target
that was unreachable for me. Plus, it was also quite a costly investment.
But mostly, I thought I wasn't smart enough or good enough to go for it.
When I asked her, "What do you think, should I go for this? Do you really
think I can do it?" She instantly said, "Yes, of course you can, absolutely."

I will always be grateful to her, as she believed in me at a time when I
wasn't one hundred percent confident in my own capabilities. She helped
me take my next big decision, and it was a big mountain indeed.

This was a much more complex and lengthier course. It's an official professional qualification. You can open your own practice once you have successfully completed the whole course and have the relevant experience.

It covered not just complex accounting processes, but also business law, taxation, business analysis models, governance and audit procedures. It consisted of three modules, 14 papers altogether, and three hours writing at the exams. To get ready for each paper, there were a lot of lectures that I had to attend, and plenty of studying I had to fit in. I was a single mother, working in a demanding environment, going to college at night after work and studying afterwards at home, alongside all the other responsibilities.

I could not take on more than four papers per year, as the examination was twice a year, around June and December. Two topics at the time was already a big load for me. I had so many balls to juggle in my early 30s.

Thinking back, one of the best outcomes of the decision I took to pursue this accreditation was, that in that process, I happen to have met some new amazing souls. These people are still in my life to this day and are the kind of friends I call family. It took me four years to go through all the exams and that came with some sacrifice.

Firstly, when it came to my son, as I literally had to lock myself into my bubble and focus on intense studying for at least a couple of weeks before each exam. I was feeling guilty for not being able to spend more quality time with him, without thinking about the content I had to cover. He needed his mum and I know that I wasn't there as much as I wanted to be and should have been during these times.

Secondly, I had to turn down all my friends who asked me to go to the beach, or go for coffee or to the movies. I was constantly adjusting my entire life around that goal for almost four years. I stayed very focused and organised with my studies, but it paid back in the end. When I think back to the whole thing, I wonder how I did it!

One of my close buddies who was taking these exams at the same time as me, always sang my praises when I passed each paper. I can still hear him saying, "How are you able to do this? You are a single mother, a career woman, you have so many responsibilities at work and at home and you pass every paper, while some of us have none of your challenges and still can't pass all the exams?" It made me smile every time I heard him say that. I guess I somehow managed to focus my energy and I felt quite connected with everything that was happening around the exams.

Now that I think about it, I also had some very special help every now and then. I must share with you this experience I had, just around one of these examinations. I don't know if you believe in dreams, but I do. Many of us receive intuitive messages during sleeping states. My channel for intuition seems to be dreams. Not always, but many times.

I always get curious and try to decode them, especially if I can still remember specific details after waking up. I strongly believe that any information we receive via any means of intuition is important to us at that time. I recall every morning for three consecutive days, waking up and remembering my dreams. On the third morning, I opened my eyes, and realised that, for three nights in a row, I had dreamt about various colleagues from work.

I was still in bed sleepy, trying to untangle why I was seeing these people and what the dream was trying to tell me. Then, I suddenly found something the visions had in common. All people, both men and women, had names that began with the letter 'S'. Every single one of them. The letter S from the English alphabet is pronounced SIGMA in the Greek language and looks like this: "Σ". While processing all of this in my head, my eyes started to open wider, and then another thing clicked.

I was studying for an examination on a paper about business analysis and project management. There was a chapter in this book about a business model called "The Six Sigma". This is a well-known six-step project management tool used with the aim of reducing the margin of defects, errors or waste in a business. Up to that point, I hadn't had really covered that chapter in much detail; I had just briefly gone through it.

I jumped out of bed and started looking for my book to find that chapter. I was thinking to myself, "Imagine if this topic is a potential part of the examination?" I mean this book was one of the most voluminous out of all 14 papers, and there was so much information to cover. There was no way of knowing what would be examined, so you had to have a good knowledge on everything, and that was pretty much impossible.

Needless to say, that I covered that chapter fully at that point and made sure I understood it properly, just in case.

On the day of the exam, I sat at the desk in the huge assessment hall, with the document closed in front of me, waiting with my heart in my throat for the examiner to give the green light. When I opened the paper, I slowly turned page by page, to review the main topics and to plan my approach on how to "attack it" because every second counted.

I could not believe my eyes when, on the last page, for 25 marks out of the 100 targets, there was a full essay on The Six Sigma. In that moment, I didn't feel like jumping up and screaming "YES". Instead, I had this strange feeling: I wasn't sure if the exam even mattered anymore. I just wanted to drop on my knees and cry. I felt such a powerful connection with the universe or God or whatever you want to call it. Now if that was not a miracle, what was it?

I wiped off my tears with my sleeve, and started to write. Three hours later, when it was over, my neck was nearly locked, and I could not feel my fingers from all the writing. I left the examination room feeling so blessed it was unbelievable. Of course, a month or so later when the results were out, it turned out that I had passed. However, let me tell you, if I hadn't had the dream to point me toward that chapter, it would have been a fail. I have learnt to always follow my intuition and it hasn't let me down yet. It's only when we don't, that we regret things in life.

Fast forward a few years and many more exams, and I had acquired my second professional qualification, this time as a Chartered Certified Accountant. This achievement happened while I was also working for one of the "big four" firms at that time, excelling at my job, managing between being a single parent and a demanding work environment and handling large portfolios of international business clients.

The universe is magical and, it answered all my prayers. Things I had only dreamt of a few years back, were real now. I was independent, I had a secure job and a very good income for a single parent. It was almost equal, to the average income of a couple.

My son was doing great as well. By that time, I had enrolled him to a private school. I remember at one of the parent teachers meetings, the tutor was telling me how good he was at school. "As much as I want to, I can't take all the credits for that. He does most of the studying on his own now. I used to help him when he was little, but not anymore", I replied. It really touched me when he continued: "That may be true, but you deserve all the credit for raising him and building that strong foundation, which is evident in his overall behaviour."

One of the things that I had always found amusing as my son was growing up, is that everywhere we went together, people never knew he was my son.

I remember one time as we were passing through the customs at the airport, one of the passenger agents there heard him calling me mum during our conversation. He then stopped me and said: "Excuse me madam, I hope you don't mind me asking, did he just call you 'mum'?" Yes, I replied as the corners of my mouth turned up into a smile. "But how is this possible, I mean biologically possible? You have to share your secret madam, this is just incredible", he voiced astounded. That always made us both smile.

Everything was great. I was living my dream. I could afford more than a decent life. Private high school for my son and our little luxuries. Life was so good to us. What had once been an impossible dream, had become reality.

FINDING MY CALLING

My boat was beautifully floating on the river; the sun was shining and the birds were chirping. The sun rays were kissing my face as I was riding my boat, and I could see the sparkles reflected in the water, shining like precious stones. There was no sign of any storms ahead and the old storms were just a vague memory. On the bank of the river, the willow tree was gently dancing with the breeze and its branches playing with the sunrays, making soft swooshing sounds, like whispers of a beautiful song.

It almost felt like it was the first time I had truly noticed its soothing, grounding presence. But at the same time, I knew that it had always been somewhere in the background of my life watching out for me ever since I was a little child. My soul was smiling with gratitude and taking in every bit of that moment.

Years flew by and my son was already a young man. Before I knew it, he was already 18. He had just passed his driving test. I remember one day when he was telling me how his classmates, all the 7th grade guys, were driving all sorts of expensive cars to school. Most teenagers there, came from wealthy families, so they could probably afford that easily. Nevertheless, just like most parents, I felt fortunate to be able to support my child through private school.

I remember this conversation we had one day, because I realised that, there comes a time when they're suddenly all grown up and will naturally want or need more.

After I had listened to him telling me how this guy at school drove an expensive car, the brand of which I will refrain from mentioning, I asked him: "If money were not an issue at all, and I could get you any car you want tomorrow, what do you think I would do? Do you think it would be smart or necessary to get something that extravagant at this point?"

He swiftly answered, "No of course. I know you would not get me something ridiculously expensive. There is no point. All I need is a safe car to get around. I can buy my own dream car when I get older and have my own job."

He was always very reasonable, even when little, but at that point, I knew I did a decent job raising him. And of course, I bought him a beautiful car which he drove safely everywhere he wanted.

I had done the best I knew to create a healthy environment for both of us to flourish. They say that your life is always influenced by the people that you surround yourself with and that's very true. I always felt, and still do to this day, that my life was always filled with wonderful people.

One very dear friend, who had known me at my lowest point when I was still stuck in a bad marriage and heartbroken, said something that stayed with me until this day:

"I am so glad to finally see you happy. I remember years ago, when you were so sad and worried, pushing your little boy in the stroller with your head down. You were like a seed blown by the wind and lost in the dust. But you found the nourishing ground and the strength to sprout and now you've blossomed into this magnificent flower, for everyone to admire."

She was spot on. This pretty much summed it all up to that point.

From the day I got married in 1992 until 1999, I had been through seven years of tremendous emotional and physical storms. I had also been blessed to become a mother and that had changed my life forever.

After the divorce in the year 2000 and throughout the next ten years until 2010, everything in my life started to shift. I was ascending continuously, in all aspects of my life.

To sum it all up, when I had chosen life on my own, back in 2000, I was feeling like a total wreck, both physically and emotionally and it was evident in all aspects of my life. I had been mentally traumatized, physically abused and I was scared not knowing what the future would bring. I did not have any professional qualifications or savings and had a little coconut to look after as well.

Looking back to this period of ten years, it appeared as if I had been climbing up a ladder at a constant pace and everything had magically fallen into place. From below zero, fast forward ten years later, and I found myself in a beautiful flat, with a panoramic view of the city. I had built up a career with a great job that could support more than just our needs, but a comfortable life as well. The fears and wounds from the past began to dissipate. I felt financially secure, free and independent. I felt confident and happy. I can say without a doubt that life had given me everything I had asked for to that point.

They say "Only look back, to see how far you have come." Very true. I had flashbacks of memories from the stormy days of my marriage. Lying my head on the pillow, with tears sliding down my cheeks while my heart was inundated with sorrow, humiliation, guilt, and entrapment when all I wanted was freedom. Freedom to live a happy and peaceful life with my son. And now, I was living it.

During all these years, my family had been very supportive and we were lucky enough to see each other often. We'd either travel to see them or they would come to visit us. It was always great being around each other and feeling the love and connection.

My little sisters were not little anymore. They had their own families too. It's funny when you think about it. My middle sister married a Swedish man and moved to Sweden and my little sister married an English guy and moved to UK. All of us have somehow spread across Europe, leaving my mum and dad with an empty home. It was and still is, difficult for them to be alone back in Romania. Luckily, we get to see each other often enough, thanks to the media channels for communication nowadays.

Ever since my son had been old enough to look after himself, I had felt like I could begin to live my own life as well. It's almost as if I had given myself permission to do something just for me.

Every so often, I'd always had this feeling that I had lost precious time with my sisters because I left home so young. We didn't get to do much fun stuff together, just the three of us. To make up for that, we'd frequently make plans and organised short getaways together.

We've travelled to places in Europe we've never been before and even to the US at one point. It was always great to be together, being laid-back without a worry in the world, and just bond and enjoy that much needed sisters time. It always seemed to just fly by so quickly.

When your family is spread across different countries it's a great feeling when you finally get together. I remember the Christmas and New Year of 2010/2011 was the best ever! All our family was gathered together and we all spent our Christmas holidays at my place. It was an extra full house and it created the best memories. I think it was the first time in years when all my immediate family and my nephews had been in one place. Such great times.

Just after high school, my son had to serve in the army for two years, after which we were planning that he would go to the university in the UK, where my little sister was living at that time. He had decided to study engineering, but he had to serve first. Two years of national service was a long time, and challenging for him. He was promoted to sergeant in the air force control, and having a higher rank elevated him a bit mentally.

Living by myself for the first time in my life at 37 felt strange at the beginning. I was looking forward to seeing him over the weekends and that would sometimes only be twice a month. I was enjoying my freedom. And a sparkling clean home never hurt anyone to be honest, though it felt less lively without him.

Most of my time was dedicated to working on my career. I felt life was so good to me: I was healthy; my son was well; I had a great job, great friends and a beautiful home. I was living my dream.

But just when you think that you have reached your ultimate goal and have all you wanted, it is amazing how life brings something else to your attention. It is almost as if it disagrees with you settling for something less than you deserve, and telling you, "It's time to make a change and expand more". And, of course, it leaves you with the challenging job of finding out for yourself what that might be.

Not easy at all. However, I believe that it is in those moments of uncertainty, doubt and cloudiness that you really have a chance to shape your destiny.

So, I sat down with myself and took stock of what I had achieved in my life, where I had been before and where I had arrived. What I realised was that, most of the choices that I'd made to that point had been to undo past mistakes. It had been about taking life into my own hands and raising my son, to offer him everything that I knew he deserved.

I realised that my choice of what I was doing for a living, building a career in the world of finance and tax, had been driven by the need for security. Anyone who is raising family and kids would look for the same thing, especially a single parent like myself. It wasn't easy, but it was very rewarding at the same time. It gave us what we needed, I loved what I was doing and was good at it too. I had many responsibilities, projects and a team to work with.

However ultimately, my work life started to get so busy, to the point where it always felt like a day was not enough to complete the work that had to be done. Every day I felt like I was going to a battle, trying to survive the day. I was constantly multi-tasking, trying to keep all those balls up in the air. If you work in the financial, banking or advisory industry, I'm sure you can relate to this.

The problem is that you are constantly in flight or fight mode, doing everything automatically. You focus on every aspect of the business, so you don't miss anything. You spend so much energy in your head and you completely forget to synch with your heart. All this is unfolding while you have no clear idea of where your future is heading, because you don't have time to think about that. In addition, you don't eat well, you lose energy, you skip exercise because you have deadlines, and you end up not having a normal private life.

This is what the rat race is all about. Wake up, go to work, push hard, go home, eat some food, maybe drink some wine, then sleep and repeat it all again.

I remember being always the last to rush into my gym classes at the end of the day. It all began to feel overly stressful. When I had a bit of time to think about my future, I could not see myself going up that corporate ladder for some reason. I noticed that all these years I had been climbing a ladder that was leading me to the wrong place. It felt like it wasn't meant for me. I was looking up but did not want to continue climbing. Everything up to this point had been driven by a clear vision. That is exactly what had got me so far. Now, I felt like I was coming to a crossroads and I knew there would be a moment where I had to decide which way to go.

One Sunday mid-morning, I was in the office alone. The week would go by so quickly, it seemed that weekends were the only times when I could do my own work in peace at the office, quietly without any interruptions.

My son was serving in the army at the time, so there was not much else for me to do at home. I realised that I was officially married to my job.

As I was typing and watching my computer screen at work that morning, with the windows open for fresh air, I could hear loud chatter and music coming from outside. A nice breeze of air and a warm feeling came to me. I remembered it was carnival time and people were getting ready to party and march that day. Then I paused, thinking, "Wait a minute; wasn't I here this time last year… OMG and the year before? Why am I not out there with my friends?"

That is when I asked myself, "Okay wait, where are you going? Where do you see yourself a few years from now?" I didn't know exactly where I wanted to be in a few years' time, but I immediately knew that I didn't want to be there doing that. I knew that there had to be a better way to live your life and have a job that offers you security and satisfaction at the same time, without having to pay such a price.

So, there I was, recognizing that I need to move on, and to take a different direction. At the same time, I was trying to figure out what my calling was.. "Where should I go from here?" I knew there was something else that I was meant to be doing but could not figure out what that was.

The first time around, my decision was easy. I wanted security. It was obvious. Now, I wanted to make a choice, and there was no gun pointed at me. It felt like a totally different place to be deciding from.

A part of me was telling me, "You can't do this now; you have worked all your life for this. You made so many sacrifices and you are so close." And then I asked myself "Close to what?" The level of stress was definitely not worthwhile. By the time I would have got "there", I'd probably be a wreck. Besides, it felt like my soul was pulling me in a totally different direction. Not long after, it turned out to be the elephant in the room, but I could not see it unfolding, until I was ready to see it. Then something funny happened one late afternoon.

As I was going to the gym, someone stopped me on the street to ask me what kind of professional sport I was involved in. They thought they knew me from TV or something. I smiled and thanked them.

Later, when I got there and was getting ready for my class, someone thought I was the fitness instructor and asked me a few fitness-related questions. When I told her that I was an accountant, she said, "That is so inspirational, that means there is hope for all of us who want to look like you."

There had been countless similar occasions over the years and it had always made me smile, but I had never paid attention or taken it seriously. I've always had an athletic allure and people were very generous with their compliments, but I never allowed myself to receive it in a different way.

I remember walking into the office after going to the gym in the mornings and everyone telling me that I filled the space with a new energy.

My manager was always teasing me saying, "What pills did you take this morning, can I have some?!" I'd always bring in bottled water, which I kept # under my desk, and had healthy snacks with me as well. Everyone was watching and commenting on my lifestyle and healthy diet. But I just did not make anything out of it. That's why I said earlier that it was like the elephant in the room. It was so deeply rooted in my daily habits that I could not even see it. It was like brushing my teeth every day. But I had never paid attention to it. Not until that time.

As I was driving home and thinking about the day's experiences, something clicked. How could I have not thought about it before? It had been there all the time, but I had been too focused on other things and had not seen it. I had been living in my head, thinking about work, the next thing I needed to do, and what bills I needed to pay.

It seemed that my true calling had always been whispering to me, but I could only hear it when I was ready. How amazing is life, when such things happen to you?

That evening, especially after all the happy hormones from the exercise, I understood what a big part of my life fitness and wellness were. My mind started to bring back memories and snippets of things that had happened in the past, which I had never thought of before.

I remember one of my teammates, said to me one day, "What are you doing in here? You should be somewhere out there facing people and sharing all this good energy with them. You're wasting your qualities here behind this screen".

It's funny how, when you become aware of something, your mind just keeps bringing you more and more information about it. I laid my head on my pillow that night thinking about all of it.

When I walked into the office the next day, I noticed that many colleagues had bottled water on their desks. This hadn't been the case when I started to work there a few years earlier. Some of them even had almonds and dried fruits; when I looked up, someone was just walking in holding a pack of bottled water from the store. I smiled.

Later that day, my manager came and asked me for some healthy snacks. He knew I always had some. I suddenly had another "wake-up" moment.

Is it possible to influence people without even trying, merely by walking your own path? Was it possible that I might have influenced these people to live more healthily, just by living my life according to my personal beliefs and values?

This was a great realisation for me: something I had never considered before.

STRAIGHT DIVE

E ating nutritious food and performing plenty of physical activity had always been a major part of my lifestyle. That doesn't mean I was not indulging or treating myself. But I've always believed in balance, so I was eating all kinds of food, so long as it wasn't too much of it.

Physical activity played a great deal in my wellbeing and mental health, especially through the stressful stages of my life. In fact, it had been my anchor during all the storms I had been through. It always gave me a big breath of freshness, positive energy, and a clear mind. And I really needed that last one.

The more I thought about it, the more I found myself tempted to step out of my comfort zone. I was slowly starting to drift away from a job that offered me financial security, towards something that was unknown and made no sense whatsoever. It was certainly nowhere near as secure in any aspect. I had one foot on the ground and another in the water. Somehow water felt different, better, excitingly uncertain. I knew I might get soaked, but it felt right.

Without having a particular plan, I decided to give up on "the bird that was eating from my palm, for another one that might or might not even come close to me". I was ready to give up the nine to five security for a dream. How crazy is that?! But it was closer to who I really was. It felt like the best expression of myself in life at the time.

There I was, one more time, finding myself at zero again. Willing to start all over. The difference now, as opposed to my past decisions, was that I wasn't desperate. I wasn't forced to do it. I didn't have a little baby whose life and future depended on me.

I felt free and I was following a whisper that came from my heart. In addition, for the first time it felt like I was changing the course of my life by a natural choice and not because I had to. This was a calling, a spiritual choice you make based on that same value.

This sense of inner spiritual guidance, was something I felt I had since I was little. I did not know what being spiritual really felt like, or meant back then, but I've always had a sense of reassurance and calmness that came from within, whenever I was worried or afraid of something. It was like a shelter within myself and it always felt comforting. This time, I knew exactly what it was. It was my inner compass, and I felt compelled to follow it.

Needless to say, I was sharing all my thoughts and what was going on in my life with my family all the time. My sisters always knew everything that I was going through, and the other way around. Even though we were all miles apart, we were always just a phone call away.

Of course, they encouraged me to follow my dreams. My little sister, who wasn't so little anymore, had also had a son as well, my nephew and second godson by the way. She is very good at technology and she offered to help me put up a wellness and fitness website to support me. She also offered to do some research on everything that was needed for that part of the project.

I started to look up ways to obtain a recognised professional qualification in fitness. I found this course from a well-known association in USA, California. Without a second thought, I signed up. It was an online course and I could take my own time to study and decide when I want to take the final exam. It worked like magic.

I was so excited when I began to study Sport Sciences and Nutrition. It felt nothing like the other academic studies I had undergone in the past. I enjoyed every single bit of it. It was very interesting and pleasing to solidify my passion for healthy living with an official qualification. Not long after, I felt proud to officially receive my professional accreditation as a Specialist in Fitness Nutrition and Fitness Trainer with a special distinction.

That meant I could apply all my knowledge and experience to help anyone with fitness and nutrition advice. It was official. So here I was, at a crossroads, changing my career to follow my passion. New chapter, new beginning. I will never forget the moment I walked out of the office building for the last time. It's never easy to say goodbye to something that was part of your life for a decade, but my conviction and deep knowing that I was following my calling, made the transition feel easy and right.

By that time, my son had finished his service in the army and the next thing: he was off to university in the UK. It was a big change and very difficult for me when he moved abroad, but I was very pleased for him for getting where he was. Like any parent, I was worried that he was far away, but the thought of my little sister being close to him, gave me a sense of reassurance and that put my mind at ease. Our home didn't feel much like home anymore, it was too quiet, something was missing. Suddenly it all seemed different.

Everything happened so fast and, in a short while, my website was up, my business cards were printed and my diary was booked. Everyone that knew me was congratulating me for having the courage to do what I did. Most of them were already keen to find out all my secrets for keeping so well physically. Word of mouth works best and, when I coupled this with a good presence on social media, it was done! I was in business.

I began to work with some associates, renting a place within a health centre facility, in which to train my clients. I was offering health packages like nutrition and training plans and group classes. Everything was happening effortlessly and it felt very natural to me. It was like I had been doing it forever. Clients were happy and rapidly seeing progress.

From that moment on, my life was about helping people to gain back their self-confidence, passion and zest for life. Since I have walked quite a long distance in those shoes, I knew there was a way to have a balanced healthy lifestyle, even in times of storms and challenge.

I have helped many people and guided them through their physical transformations. I felt fortunate to have the privilege of making a difference in one's life and to experience all the wonderful, unique sentiments that come with that. This made me realise that true fulfilment comes from doing whatever supports being true to yourself.

Everything was going smoothly and life seemed so "light" in Cyprus with my new passion. They say that if you love what you do, you never have to work a day in your life. True. It never felt like work and it still doesn't.

Needless to say, that this career shift was radical; it was in a totally different direction. Each day would go by so easily and it was incredible how rested I felt at the end of it. There's nothing like being your own boss and having your own diary. Waking up in the morning, wearing a light gym kit, putting your shades on, driving to the club to make people sweat and getting paid for it: how did I get so lucky?

It felt like such an easy, joyful living. The programs, classes and all the creativity around it, was such an effortless thing. I was enjoying every moment of it. It never felt like work, in fact it felt like play. And at the same time, I was making just about the same money, but working half of the time that I had been putting into the office before, and, most importantly, experiencing ZERO stress levels.

I was thinking about it at one point, really trying to remember how I had been living with that amount of stress all these years. Honestly, it seemed like I was living another life.

Back in the UK, my son was doing well with his studies. I remember him telling me that the private school helped him a lot, as he could understand everything so much better than other fellow students who were struggling.

My little sister in UK was going through her own storms at the time. She needed help with weight loss. She became a vegetarian, so I put together a tailored vegetarian diet plan for her and suggested targeted exercise. A year later she was 20 pounds lighter.

One time when I was there to visit her and my son as well, we talked about setting up a proper wellness business in UK. We were having coffee in the morning and, before you know it, we were sharing ideas for new business plans and how to scale it, drawing stuff on pieces of paper.

It was just ideas at the time. We were thinking out loud and it seemed like a brilliant idea, to be honest. The only thing was, that it implied me moving to UK and I wasn't really ready to give a decisive answer at that time. Besides, it was just over a year since I had made the big shift in my career. I wasn't ready for another major change.

I returned to Cyprus and continued to practice what I loved in my safe environment. Everything was going well and it felt good, but it also began to feel small. I remember this one morning while I was doing my cardio riding a stationary bike looking at my reflection in the mirror; I had a strange feeling that there was more for me. I felt limited in a sense I could not quite put my finger on at that time. I didn't give it too much thought, but I think it stayed in the back of my mind.

The next day, I went for a run by the beach just before sunrise. It was always magical. The sense of freedom that it gave me could not compare with anything. I continued with my usual my daily routines, ticking everything off my diary with ease.

A short while after my visit to UK, my sister asked me again if I had thought about the business idea. I think I was still avoiding it. I knew that it was going to be such a big change; I would have had to start my life all over again.

The thought of the change was scary for many reasons: the economy, quality of life, pollution, travelling, food, and the fitness industry, which I suspected may be approaching the point of saturation. I wasn't sure if I could succeed and make our dreams happen. I was scared.

But I could not avoid it anymore. I had to sit down, face my fears and be honest with myself. On the surface, I had all these thoughts about the implications of changing my lifestyle. For instance, all my life I had been driving my own car, living in a paradise where most of the year is sunny. I loved that small city, the palms, the beach, my little luxuries, my home, and my little baby business that I had just given birth to. I had many attachments there.

On the other hand, I loved the thought of living with my sister and my nephew and be reunited again. My son was also in the UK, and I would be close to him as well. The idea of reaching more people and making an impact at a bigger scale was also tempting despite the fact that my confidence was a bit low in that respect at the time. But it didn't take too long, and the day came when I actually had to sit down and take a decision.

I recall that day very clearly. It was a day when I decided to face my fears and be truthful with myself. I sat by my kitchen table, lit a candle and took a piece of paper and a pen.

Then I asked myself:

What is it that keeps you from leaving this place?
What is it that you don't want to let go of?
Why can't you make up your mind?

The moment I asked myself those questions, I started writing and writing as my tears fell onto that paper.

It was so hard to leave behind everything that I had built with so many struggles. The thought of leaving all my friends was heartbreaking. I was so fortunate and blessed beyond my imagination with many wonderful people in my life. They were my family and I was theirs. I could not find it in myself to leave them behind. How can you leave behind a lifetime of friends? I had lived there for 22 years.

How could I leave the place where I had given birth to my son? The place I had raised him and the place I had truly grown up myself. It was the place where I had fallen in love with life, and which had brought peace to my mind and soul. I used to sit by the beach there and hear the waves talking to me. I had taken magical morning runs by the beach and experienced total freedom and a deep connection with the sea and all parts of nature there. How can you leave a place you call home, a place you found serenity, a place that has become your sanctuary?

I figured that these were the reasons why I could not make up my mind. There was too much history and emotion attached to it all. I stopped writing but the tears were still helping all those emotions to find their way out.

I then started to remember how sad and depressed I had been when I was unhappily married: how I could feel and hear the vibration of existence and people enjoying life while I was just trapped in a glass bubble, unable to reach outside.

I remembered how hard it had been to get up, get in that driver seat and take the wheel of life in my own hands and raise my son on my own. I remembered how I had started from the dust, (as one of my friends had described it) and made my way, ascending slowly, step by step, just like I had dreamed of doing.

I remembered how blessed I was and how life had offered me everything that had once been a dream. I remembered that with faith, and love under my wings, I had risen above all the storms in my life. I remembered that I found the joy and happiness I once thought I'd lost forever. I was well, healthy, living my life and following my dreams. My son was studying at university following his dreams too. I felt utterly blessed that life had been good to both of us.

When the tears dried out, I had such clarity of mind. It was like all the clouds began to part and the sun started to shine through. It felt like my mind was clear and my soul was light. I realised that, at the core of everything, home is where your heart is. It doesn't matter what part of the world you are in, if your intentions are clear and you put passion and love into whatever it is that you do, it will always feel like home.

Once again, I felt grateful for every soul that crossed my path, for every life that had touched mine and for every life that I may have touched in turn to that point. I felt so blessed to have had friends that I could call family and thankful to the whole universe for unfolding my life in such a wonderful, miraculous way.

That's when I finally made my decision. I was ready to take another leap and hope to God that everything would work out.

LEAVE IT ALL BEHIND AND START AGAIN

I t was fascinating to notice how my energy had shifted in my body again. Once I'd made up my mind, I had a vivid sense of clarity and direction and I needed all of it.

There was so much to be done. Packing up 22 years of life is not easy, but somehow it went like clockwork. I sat down beforehand and used my detailed planning skills. I listed all the items I had, from vehicles to kitchen supplies and clothes.

Next, I simply put it all into action. I reached out to all my friends and people I knew well to let them know that I was giving away all these things, just to see if they were interested so that I could take it to the next level. I already had in mind who might want my things, and it was easier than I thought. So much so, that in one week everything was done. I sold our cars in two days. People responded so swiftly.

When it came to the final bits like kitchenware, home decorations, clothes and shoes (of which I had plenty, too many, to be honest) I decided to give it all away to close friends. I'm not going to lie, I was a bit of a fashion freak and the irony was that I liked expensive stuff. Nevertheless, I could not take it all with me and it was the perfect time to declutter.

I decided to organise an afternoon tea party where I displayed everything I had for all my close ladies' friends. They were pleased to get some of my good stuff. I was smiling when they were telling me "I have had my eye on this one for a long time". That is exactly why I did not want to give them to strangers or a second-hand shop. It had more of an emotional value for me, as well as for them, since they would get something to remind them of me.

It was incredible to count 60 pairs of high heels and 30 pairs of trainers I had lined up in the flat. And that doesn't even include the boots and other styles of shoes! I literally had my head in my hands when I looked at it all. There were things I had even forgot I had. They looked brand new, still in the shoe boxes as I had barely worn them. It's incredible to grasp how much of our financial resources go on things we barely use. In the end, of course, I decided to keep only the things I loved, which filled three big luggage cases; that's all I wanted to keep.

One more time, I witnessed the power of the universe. Everything worked like magic. When you make up your mind, all your energy shifts and things around you just align as you need them. I wished that it was all; but there was more, and I wasn't keen on that part.

The hardest thing I ever had to do, was to say goodbye to all the people that I loved: my friends, my clients and everyone that was part of my life. At the end of the party when they all had to leave, I remember holding those hugs for so long and crying together. Our emotions were not even verbalised; there was no need and we could barely speak anyway.

In a way, this experience reminded me of another time in my life where I had felt the same thing when I had to say goodbye to people I loved deeply. That had been when I was 18 and had decided to leave my hometown, get married and move abroad. This time I was in my 40s.

And just like that, I packed up 22 years of life, and moved on to new adventures in the big city of London in March 2015. It was really difficult to leave that place with all my life packed into three bags; my heart filled with so many sentiments and a lifetime of experiences.

But at the same time, it was quite exciting. I was fortunate to have family by my side. It would have been much harder to go through such a change all alone again.

I didn't waste much time to compare the life I had before with the new one. I was tempted to, but that would have achieved nothing. It was like comparing apples with pineapples. What I did instead was this: every time I'd catch myself going that way, I'd be open to embrace the new. Besides, how do you compare moving from a very small city by the seaside with a population of somewhere short of 200.000 people, to a huge multicultural city of 8.6 million people at that time.

This scale clearly influences the quality of life. I have to confess, it was very challenging to adjust to everything at the beginning. From the quality of food to the weather, lifestyle, travelling and commuting. I knew I gave up the independence and the little luxury of driving my own vehicle around easily and getting to places in no time. London is not a city you want to be driving in through the rush hour, so getting around was a whole new experience. I used to feel like an alien every time I jumped on a crowded bus or tube. Not to mention the fact that it was all so confusing.

My sister always giggled when I was rolling my eyes in the tube or trying to figure out the journey on my own. On the other hand, it was great to be reunited with my family and to be closer to my son as well. The idea of a new beginning and new opportunities in this big city was exciting and that kept me going.

From the very start, in the first few months after I moved to the UK, I decided to join a gym, as a client. Exercise is like a necessity for me. My sister, with whom I was living at the time, suggested a health club that was just around the corner from where we lived, so it worked perfectly.

I was there every day, so the staff started to notice me, and knew me well after a little while. One day, the fitness manager of the club, approached me and told me that they were holding interviews for a new position as a personal trainer. She asked me if I was interested.

At that time, it was very soon after I've moved and I was still figuring out how to go about our business idea. So, I discussed it with my sister and decided to take the opportunity. I was looking forward to getting an insight into how the fitness industry worked in the city and I knew the money would be useful as well. Plus, I could earn it by practicing my passion and spending my time in a pleasant way.

I was pleased to have passed the interview with flying colours, as I was told later. It was a full day of activities that involved specific practical and interpersonal skills. Did I feel outside of my comfort zone? Absolutely! I was stretching way out of it. A part of me was worried that maybe I wasn't good enough for what they expected of me, while another part was whispering "just do your best and that should be enough". The best things in my life had always happened when I acted despite all fears. This was no different.

There was a new health club opening in London and I got good references for that position. It was one of the top health clubs in UK, owned by a famous public figure. The place was right in the middle of everything, walking distance from the famous Tower Bridge, near which we were living at the time.

Fast forward a year and half, and there I was in my 40s, working for one of the classiest health clubs in London. In the beginning, when we were all getting to know each other, most of my peers were shocked when I told them my actual age. When I also told them, I had a son who was old enough to have a girlfriend, they would almost swear at me. It was always entertaining to see their astonishment. It made me laugh every time. And even though I felt self assured in general, it was a nice extra boost for my confidence.

I was getting along well with all my colleagues, the new life in the fitness environment and was even slowly beginning to feel the pulse of the city. It was such a great experience to be able to have access to and learn all about the latest trends in the fitness technology. This included high-performance treadmills and stationary bikes, and how to prepare for and train people in altitude chambers. We had one of these rooms in the club. It's also known as a hypoxic chamber, which simulates high altitudes, more precisely the air composition that you would breathe at the top of a mountain.

This way of training helps to improve fitness performance and also gives great health benefits. Most performance athletes train in these surroundings to prepare for better results. One of the effects of training in these environments is an increase in the production of red blood cells, which in turn helps with an increased rate of transportation of nutrients and energy through the body, which improves physical performance.

Everything was new and it all seemed so cool and exciting. The managers of the club sang my praises from the start. It felt awesome to be nominated star of the first month and see my name on that honour panel. I was happy to be classified amongst the top trainers in the club. I don't even know how two years went by so quickly.

I had learnt so much about the fitness industry and gained so much valuable experience during this time. I felt really fortunate to be in that environment. I can tell you without a shadow of a doubt that my confidence as a fitness coach and a wellness representative was significantly boosted. And that was because I was interacting with all these people and conditions in that space. The best part was that I met many wonderful people while working there. Most of them I still interact with to this day and a few are as close as family.

We were living 20 minutes away from my workplace, so I did not even have to use public transport to commute. Again, I felt fortunate. I could walk there every day, while other colleagues had to travel for hours to get to the health club in the centre of the city. Public transport is still something that I struggle with. I guess I'm not a Londoner at heart.

However, I also have to reveal the other side of the coin. While I enjoyed every moment, it was quite demanding and it involved considerable effort to meet or exceed the monthly targets. The system was designed to encourage you to work harder if you wanted to get paid better. However, even so, the salary was still small, compared to what I used to receive back in Cyprus, and even to what other self-employed professionals, were earning in the city.

To give you an idea, if you were a high performer, you could get a maximum of 34% of what a client paid for your hourly services. The remaining 66% went to the club. That's the catch when you work for a well-established gym chain, where you don't pay any rent for the space you use. I was delivering services worth £9k per month for the club, and

I was getting less than a third of that, before taxes. And it's no secret that tax rates in UK are crazy.

Luckily, I was busy enough and could get by, but even so, in terms of numbers, I was going backwards. My bank account wasn't too healthy. After almost two years of long hours, waking up at 5 am, early sessions starting 6.30 am on Monday mornings, it began to feel like the financial rewards didn't match the efforts. I felt a bit stuck, as if I was not moving forward. Luckily, I was living with my sister and she was covering most of the living costs, as I was still also supporting my son through university at that time.

On the other hand, I was doing much research for our own business, so I could gather information and explore ways to get it started. I was often quite exhausted after a full day at the gym. My sister had her own job as well, in the banking sector. The time came when I had to do a trade-off and weigh up the benefits and costs.

In April 2017, I decided to stop working for the health club, and to focus all my energy and time trying to find a way to integrate our own business ideas into the fitness industry. It was already two years since I had moved and I was beginning to feel like I had got myself trapped somewhere, without much progress on our own business vision. I wanted to move on.

We gathered information, drew up a detailed business plan and presented it to a business angels' platform. We needed £5 million to start our business idea. Surprisingly, not long after, we had a couple of interested investors and an offer on the table. This one was a bit questionable, especially when the investor called and wanted to meet with us two days later in Italy to sign the papers and transfer £1m to begin with. That was a red flag for me.

We requested some legal advice about this proposal, and it was suggested that it was too risky to get someone involved at this stage. There was another alternative. We could test the project at a smaller scale, trying to see how each component would work individually. So, we turned the offer down and decided to start smaller.

After a long, targeted research, I found some associates, rented a place and began to offer one-to-one sessions, nutrition plans and group classes to promote our business. This was the bread and butter of the fitness business anyway. But our dream involved so much more than that. The fitness industry is constantly changing and you need to be flexible and to adjust with the trends. That is what we did, while we had put our big dream on hold.

In a very short time, I acquired a decent client portfolio and filled the majority of my available slots. My day was quite busy with group classes, private sessions, nutrition and training programs. This time, I wasn't employed by the gym as before, but I was an associate. Which meant I was paying a monthly rent to the club, and the clients were paying me directly for my services.

I was now free to choose my pricing and to have a larger range of services to offer, as opposed to just one-to-one personal training sessions. And all this was under my own brand. It was a great advantage to be able to promote my own business, which I had not been able to do before. Even though I had to pay a fair amount of monthly rent, I was still left with a decent amount in my bank account.

There was indeed so much more potential in London. It felt great to help many people with their own special goals and dreams about their body and their health. Some would want to lose weight for their weddings, some would just want to look good for the summer, some would want to train for their next marathon and some just wanted to stay healthy and run around with their kids.

I was fully invested in what I was doing every day. It was natural to me and I was enjoying it. I wasn't making huge profits, but I loved what I was doing. It covered all my bills including business expenses and also the cost of renting a place and living by myself in London. Most importantly, it was also making an impact in other people's lives.

My classes were getting bigger and bigger, the diary was getting busy, and it was all going very well. I remember one day, I had a great surprise. One of the partners of the big four firm that I had worked for in Cyprus showed up at my class. She was visiting her daughter who was studying in

London at the time and she thought she'd stop by to see me and participate in the class. She had been watching me on social media.

I was so happy to see her. After the class, we went for dinner and a couple of drinks. We caught up on many things. I told her how my son had graduated and had already found a job in engineering at that time, and she told me her news about her daughter. We laughed and talked about old times. Towards the end, she said, "Bravo, you should be very proud of what you did. Everyone was talking about it. It took a lot of guts to do what you did." I smiled and thanked her, as it made me realise something.

At this point, we might have been a long way from having that dream business, but we were in a good place. I was running my own health and fitness business in London under the umbrella of our own brand. What had once been a dream was now reality. I remembered that day in Cyprus, when I had been safely running my own little business and doing my morning cardio on the bike when I suddenly had a deep feeling that there was something more for me.

That's what it was all about. I was now exposed to a much bigger number of people: busy, stressed city workers. I could influence more lives. I knew how important this part of health and fitness was for every one of them. That had been my purpose and intention when I had decided to jump off the wheel of the rat race.

When my little sister and I had decided to co-found our own brand and company, before I even moved to the UK, our aim had been to help busy people from the city find their way to a healthier life, because we knew these busy people well. Too well in fact, as we had been living in their shoes for years, and we'd experienced what a stressful life and a job in a challenging environment can do to you.

The feeling you get when someone tells you how much you have influenced, motivated and inspired them to positively transform their habits cannot be equalled or measured in any currency in the world. It brings such a beautiful sentiment seeing how you are contributing to other people's wellbeing and noticing how that adds to your own vitality as well.

AND THIS IS
WHAT IT SUMMED UP TO

Looking from the outside at all these decisions that I've shared with you so far, may seem strange to you. Getting married at 18 and all that came after, can be hard for some to grasp. At 39 years of age, I had been bold or crazy enough to radically change the course of my career, from a professional accountant with job security, to a fitness coach with no security whatsoever. Indeed, it's not something that happens often. However, it was a soul inspired decision. Did I ever regret it? Never. It was my calling. I felt compelled to honor it.

It can be indeed, not very common that a few years later, at 41, I decided to start a new life in a new city, and found myself living in one of the biggest cities in the world. Doing what I loved, working directly with people and helping them to find their physical strength, confidence and wellbeing. Most of my peers were over a decade younger than me, and some were even half of my age. Did I ever feel too old for this? Yes, it crossed my mind but it did not sink in for some reason. So, no, not really. I always felt young both in my spirit and in my body. I was never really driven by the "should" or "shouldn't" of social expectations.

According the "normal" culture, when you are in your 20s you usually go to university, to study for a professional qualification. That also comes along with having fun, drinking and partying, and generally enjoying those unique years of your life, while your parents work hard to support you. When I was at that age, I had been raising my baby boy, and going through tremendous emotional storms, while stuck in an unhappy marriage. Did I ever regret it? Some parts I could have done without, but at my core, no, I didn't.

That's because I got the best thing out of it; I was blessed to be a mother and could not imagine my life without my son. Being a mother in the way that it happened for me had shaped my personality and made me who I am. I believe our children are our greatest teachers.

Then, in your 30s, the social norm is that you should have a career, and aim to build a family. At that age, I had been going through a divorce, being a single mother, raising a child, putting him through school, studying and trying to build up a career as well. Quite a big plate for a young woman to deal with, especially with the emotional weight I was carrying. Was I scared? Yes, very much. But I was thirsty for freedom in all aspects of my life and eager to spread my wings and fly away to whatever direction my heart desired.

Finally, according to society, by the time you are in your 40s you should already be settled into a stable career, have a happy marriage, raising your kids, have a good savings account, get a mortgage and paying your taxes and pension. You should be living in a way that makes everyone around you happy: your boss, your partner, your in-laws, your mother, your friends and even neighbors.

The reality is, that by that age, many people are unhappy and find it hard to simply enjoy life. This is often because they are stuck in a job that they hate, but they keep going, because it pays the bills and supports the family. Or maybe they are going through serious family crises and even breakups. I'm not trying to put everyone in the same pot here, but many of us go through similar situations. This is a fact.

By that age, I'd already gone through a long series of struggles: a bad marriage, divorce, and a battle for financial security, so I could support my son through his education over the years, as well as my own education. I'd managed to secure a career plus a decent life for myself. I'd also had the privilege to discover my calling and followed my instinct to do what my heart was whispering. And I had the courage to take big decisions along the way, decisions that literally shaped the trajectory of my life as you can well see by now.

And that's the benefit of starting "upside down". You grow younger and wiser. You feel you have nothing to lose because you have been through it all.

Or at least, that's what I thought.

PART TWO

THE YEAR IN WHICH I LEARNT THE WISDOM OF THE WILLOW TREE

NEW YEAR'S
MONTHLY JOURNALS

Have you ever been scrolling on social media just after Christmas and noticed people posting stuff along these lines?

"Bye Bye current year, you were a ******* bitch, can't wait for the New Year…. blah blah blah."

Well, I remember doing just that at the end of 2018. I have to confess, I couldn't help wondering what had happened to these people. To be honest, whenever I came across posts like that, I'd always think to myself, "I wonder why they are so bitter about everything. I'm sure they must have had good moments as well. It can't all be bad."

Little did I know, that half way through 2019, I'd be one of them; someone who couldn't wait to put that year behind them. So much happened, too much for anyone to take, even someone who'd been through so much already.

The year of 2018 ended well. I rolled into the New Year in Sweden, at my middle sisters' beautiful home, having spent my Christmas holidays there. I felt recharged and energised on the flight back to London. It had been such a great break, and I was ready to begin the new year on the "right foot" as they say. I had many plans and new ideas for my business.

However, starting mid-January, an unexpected series of events started to unfold. It was like a little storm, that began to get bigger and then it felt like it was coming from all directions until it was out of control. At one point, it felt like a storm within layers of storms. The more you read through these events, the more you'll understand exactly why it felt like that.

To help you understand precisely what I mean, I will share the following events with you, and the highlights of what has happened month by month from January to October 2019. Time for you to take a comfortable seat. Oh, and just a quick heads-up. By the time you get to April, you may need to buckle up.

January 2019

Everything was going well with the business. It was the usual routine of a fitness coach: group classes and sessions. New clients were joining, with fresh goals, hopes and dreams for the new year. It was a busy time in the fitness calendar. I was progressing at full power and planning ahead.

One morning, as I woke up to get ready for my day, I had a weird feeling. It was the same feeling you have when you wake up and can still remember an intense sensation during a dream you had before you woke up.

I woke up remembering that I had a dream where I was sleeping, and had felt a very intense migraine in this dream. At least that's what I thought, because there was no sign of pain when I woke up. That was so strange, I thought to myself. But I carried on and I forgot about it for a while.

February 2019

I woke up one morning, rushing to get ready and get on with my day as usual. I got into the shower, when I noticed quite a few red spots on my skin, just around my rib cage area. I was blessed with good genes, and this was an unusual thing for me. It was strange, and I started wondering what it was all about. I thought it could be a rash or maybe an allergy.

Then I remembered that just the day before, I had used a new body scrub, a Christmas present from a friend. I also remembered using the steam room in the club and thought it could have had something to do with that. But that wasn't it.

When I got out of the shower, I had a better look and something didn't feel quite right. It looked a bit strange, and definitely not like a rash. The spots were very defined. It looked like something I had never seen before.

I called my GP practice, but they couldn't see me until the next day. There was no room for an appointment. I did not have private health insurance at the time either, so I waited.

I headed off to work and ticked off everything on my diary. In the evening I checked again and there were no significant changes with the spots. I was feeling well: a bit tired, but fine overall.

The real shock came when I woke up the next day. My whole torso was sprinkled with big red dots. It hit me, as I was holding my PJ's up looking at my tummy in the mirror. It can't be! This looks just like chickenpox. "No way! This isn't happening", I exclaimed to myself. I hadn't experienced this as a child.

A few hours later, it was confirmed by the GP. She suggested that I stay isolated until it all disappeared. My jaw dropped a few seconds later, when I asked how long it would take before it cleared out, and she replied "Usually four to five weeks". I was shocked. I simply could not believe it.

It was all so strange because physically I was feeling well. Now that I think about it, all was normal, except that for the previous few days, I had felt like I did not have as much stamina and was getting tired a bit easier than usual.

Thoughts about how this would impact everything in my life for the next few weeks, instantly started to flow through my mind. I felt terrible thinking about how this situation would affect my clients and my business in the coming weeks. It felt frustrating, as I had so many things lined up. I was thinking "I'm too busy for this now, come on…!" I almost felt as if someone wanted to put me to the naughty corner and there was nothing I could say or do.

There was no other option than to isolate myself, but it was so disheartening. I remember walking home after I got the news, feeling like a little dog with its tail between its legs: so disappointed. I was trying to figure out where to start, who to call first, and how to inform everyone about this situation and cancel everything that was in my diary for the next four weeks.

I was living on my own at that time, leasing a place in a lovely area in London, by the docks. The surroundings were so beautiful, but, to be honest, the apartment could have been better. I was just waiting for the lease term to end so that I could find something more suitable for my standards.

When I arrived home, I called my family to let them know about the incredible situation I had suddenly found myself in. My sister was also in shock when she found out and so was my son. By that time, he was living with his fiancée. Yes, he was all settled already! They had been seeing each other for a few years and he had proposed just before Christmas.

My family tried to comfort me with supportive words and asked me if I needed anything, since I wasn't able to go out anymore. I wanted to keep them from catching it, so I agreed that if I needed something, they could only drop it at my doorstep. Later that day, my mom also confirmed that I had not had this virus as a child. She felt sad for me, of course, and she gave me many tips on how to treat it at home.

I sat alone to calm down, took a few deep breaths, and then began to deal with all the business matters. There was much emailing, texting and calling that it took a day and a half. As I was lying in bed mentally exhausted, looking at the ceiling and trying to work out if I had missed anyone, then looking at my lists and diaries and all related notes, I felt lucky in spite of all my desolation. I was feeling grateful that at least I wasn't in pain.

Yes, it was frustrating because I hadn't planned for any of that. I hadn't seen it coming, especially when I was too busy and had many plans for my business. I was trying to read between the lines. I asked the universe, "What is this all about, what are you trying to tell me?" Then I thought, "What if I needed to have a break?"

Life happens; people get sick sometimes, it's all normal. I had to accept it and go with the flow. I knew that already. There is no way to control something like this. If you wake up one day with chickenpox, what can you do, other than let it take its course? I was almost laughing, just thinking how bizarre this was.

This experience taught me to surrender, go with the process and let things sort themselves out. It was almost as if someone wanted to remind me, "You're paddling so hard, all day you do, do and do. Take a break and go with the flow, while you rest for a while."

At that time, there was nothing I could do but have patience until it was over. I sat down and considered the positive aspects. I asked myself *how could I make the best of this?* I looked at my long lists of personal things I wanted to do and that I had never got to tick off; like meditating more, connecting with myself more, and reading all those books by my bedside that I hadn't had time to finish. I love to read about things like the science of mind-body connection, spirituality, and the source of our existence, which is something that always fascinated me. In addition, I could even lie back and watch some movies on Netflix!

With that thought, I started to shift my energy towards these things. I had plenty of time. There was no need to rush anymore. Little did I know that I was taking training sessions in patience.

While I was at home, I never had any fever, and wasn't itching as much as they say you will. I was completely covered by the spots, everywhere except my legs. It was all over my torso and face, but I wasn't suffering in any obvious way other than feeling a bit down, which was pretty normal I thought.

On the other hand, I have to confess, it was scary to look at myself in the mirror. There were days when I thought I'd never look the same and the scars would be there forever. I was constantly researching natural remedies and products that I thought might be helpful with the cicatrices, once they were healed. I knew that if I scratched or bothered them, they could become infected and leave me with permanent marks and more complications. So, I refrained from any of these temptations.

One home remedy I used, was to take dry chamomile baths. I would soak a small fresh towel in warm chamomile infused water, and gently wash my face and body every day, without rubbing. I would just press the cool chamomile compress against my skin. That helped me a lot. When the water was cool enough, I would just splash it gently on my face.

Luckily, I had my family close by; they delivered food and supplies while I would wave at them and have brief conversations from my balcony. I did not want them to be anywhere near me.

It took four weeks until I was not contagious anymore and all the spots cleared. I can't tell you how excited I was when I began to call my clients one by one and to book them in for their sessions, classes and meetings. My diary was nice and booked again.

The funny thing was that I had to wear a lot of makeup to cover the scars. This was something I hadn't usually had to do, but now I did. I have a mixed skin complexion, but it made me giggle when I got back to the club, and someone said, "You look tanned! Have you been on holiday?" I was so glad to be back and doing what I loved doing after such a forced break.

This was the first little storm of 2019, where I heard the wisdom of the willow tree whispered to me for the first time, *"Surrender, dance with me, follow the flow"*. And I did; however, little did I know that this was just a warm-up.

March 2019

Allow me to take you back around the end of November 2018, when I had this intense pain around my lower abdomen on the right side. I had never felt anything like it before. I thought it was my appendix. It was on a Friday morning, as I was getting ready for a morning photo-shoot that was part of a project my sister and I were putting together at the time.

I didn't want to cancel, so I took some mild painkillers, which was not something usual for me and went ahead with it. The pain came back and continued for a few hours later, as I was back to my schedule; it was quite intense. I was ready to go to the A&E, but it stopped later that afternoon. Nevertheless, I called my GP and arranged an appointment as soon as possible. When she saw me, she booked me for an ultrasound of my ovaries. It was booked for three months from that date, in March 2019. It seemed that this wasn't deemed as urgent, most probably because the pain was gone and I was feeling fine.

On the day of this appointment, I had no idea what would come out of it. I was looking forward to getting it done and going back to my busy schedule. However, as I was lying there, I was shocked to hear the radiologist who was performing the ultrasound saying that she could see a big cyst on my right ovary. It was approximately 7 cm and there was a smaller one on the left side. I just hadn't seen this one coming. Once she finished her examination, she said she would inform my GP and let me know of the urgent steps to follow.

When I walked out of there to get back to my sessions and plans for the day, I was feeling numb from the shock, to be completely honest. Then my mind started to analyse it. I called my sister, as she knew I had this appointment, and told her all about it.

My mind was conflicted, because I had never had serious menstrual issues nor pain. Everything had seemed to be working fine. I kept wondering how it was possible, considering the size of it, that I had never experienced any pain other for that one single day.

There was no way I could have known about it, because my monthly cycles were always like clockwork. I have to admit that, even though I was aware that this was a very common thing, I was still a bit dazed and beginning to worry. I went back to my sessions, clients and classes as usual, but at the back of my mind, I was worried about it.

Later that day, my phone rang in between sessions. It was a doctor from my GP's practice. He was calling to confirm the results, which I already knew. He also made it clear that, due to the size of the cyst, there had to be a procedure to remove it. That meant I had to have an operation. I remember beginning to shiver as I was listening to him.

It was one of these times when the strong wind makes its way through the branches of the willow tree, almost like an announcement that something is heading your way. I had felt this shivering breeze many times before, but this time it was different.

The previous times when I had this feeling, I had known that everything was going to be fine, once I decided what to do about the situation. I had been able to generate a bit of inner power to create that momentum and keep it spinning forward. However, when you come across health issues, you feel powerless. It's as if someone else has the paddles of the boat and there is nothing you can do anymore; it's too late. You can only watch. This reminded me that I have to find a way to stay calm and flow with it.

As I was still on the phone, trying to control my jitters, I saw my next client walking in. I wished I could have had a bit more time to be alone, but that wasn't possible. I had to set my feelings aside for a while and process them later. It was all happening simultaneously and I did my best to keep it together and to give her a great experience. It wasn't easy to just forget about what I had just heard, but I kept putting one foot in front of another.

I knew it well already, but it's always worth remembering that sometimes you need to get out of your bubble and remember that life isn't always just about you. It is also about all the other people in your life as well. People that are waiting for you to show up and make a difference in their lives every day.

It's about finding a way to be consistent even when you don't think you can. It's about dusting yourself down, getting up and carrying on. Not by pretending that nothing has happened, because that is denial, but by finding a way to move on, with all that has happened. It's about showing up, doing your best in the moment and knowing that you will take time to nurture yourself and "lick your wounds" after. I believe that the universe never makes mistakes and that everything is divinely orchestrated.

A week later, I had an appointment with a gynaecologist to talk about the diagnosis. She explained that it was best to make sure that the cysts were not malignant. She said we should perform a couple of tests, before we decided how to go ahead with any surgical procedure.

I was booked for an urgent appointment to have an MRI scan and some blood tests, as she suggested. Even though the waiting period for these wasn't long, it was a struggle. It took a lot of faith to keep myself positive. I kept telling myself, "I am healthy, I've always been. I can't have the thing that starts with the letter 'C'." Even the thought of it was outrageous. I could not even begin to think about it.

I was keeping myself sane by standing still every day and meditating on my health. I repeated countless affirmations. My favourite came from Louise Hay; she always made me feel calm when I heard her words. It's interesting how certain information comes to you at exactly the right time, when it's most needed.

Needless to say, I had great support from my family, close friends and everyone that was aware of it. I am so grateful for that. At the time, I didn't tell my parents. I wanted to wait for the results first. I felt there was no need to have them worrying about this, especially because they were far away.

In the meantime, around my monthly cycle, I had a headache again; this time it was real and not in my dreams. It lasted for two days. I've rarely ever had any headaches in the past. I figured it was to do with the latest finding about the ovarian cysts.

Finally, the night before the day when I would be meeting with the gynaecologist to discuss the results arrived. I'm not going to lie, it wasn't easy to stay focused on the positive and not to think the "unthinkable". I sat down in stillness, and prayed to the universe to give me good news the next day. I remember at some point, deep inside myself, I felt a sense of peace and quietness and then I fell asleep.

I woke up the next day and was getting ready to leave for my appointment. I felt a bit anxious for a moment and, as I turned my head and looked at my phone screen to make sure I left in time, my YouTube feed had a video titled "EVERYTHING IS GOING TO BE ALRIGHT". My eyes widened. In an instant, I knew without a doubt that there was nothing to worry about. I just knew it. It was a gut feeling, nothing to do with logic. I've always been inclined to trust my intuition as you know.

Of course, it was later confirmed; the results were clean. The cysts were non-malignant and that was great news. She kept telling me how lucky I was and reassured me that there was nothing to worry about when it came to the procedure. She explained how this is now done through keyhole surgery and that it is a short routine procedure. She said that the recovery would not be a lengthy process, but that it was best to be careful with the type of intensity and exercises that I performed as a fitness coach before and after the surgery. Clearly it affected my business and lifestyle. There was no date for any procedure yet. That was to be confirmed later.

But there was more. There was also a lump on my right kidney that had shown up in that same scan. Luckily it was something I already knew about. I began to explain how I had known about it for seven years, and told her the whole story.

Back in 2012, when I was still in Cyprus, I developed an infection called toxoplasmosis, caused by a parasite called toxoplasma. These parasites can come from animals like dogs and cats or unwashed salads, greens or infected meats.

It usually has no significant symptoms in adults, but with me, it had created inflammation in the lymph nodes, which I had noticed over the period of a week. Basically, I began to see little lumps everywhere on my neck, under my arms and at the groins. This meant that my immune system was compromised because, the larger lymph nodes in our body are at the groin and armpits. It got to the point when it was painful to feel the sleeve of a t-shirt rubbing against my armpit. That's how sensitive it was.

When I first saw my doctor about it, I had no clue that this was the case. I could see his worry when he sat to examine those lumps. They were on my neck, my head, under my arms, my groin, everywhere. It was like an explosion. It felt terrifying to see all that suddenly appearing everywhere.

We sat down and the first thing he asked me was if I had a pet at home. The answer was no. Then he started to write a list of particular blood tests he wanted me to have done the next day, including an ultrasound. To me, he was and still is one of the most brilliant diagnosticians you could have. When I thought he was done, at the last moment, he wrote one last line on that list, which was a blood test to identify this particular parasite. He clearly suspected that already.

The good thing was that the health system in Cyprus, a small country, was very different to the system in UK; I could do all the tests and get the results same day, without going through the emotional stress of waiting. That makes a huge difference.

The next day, I woke up, got ready and went to the clinic. We started with the ultrasound and he examined the lumps in my groin area. I was relieved when he confirmed instantly that the lumps were just inflamed lymph nodes and there was nothing to worry about. That is when the ultrasound also picked up the lump on the kidney. He diagnosed that as a lipoma. In medical terms, a lipoma is a benign growth created by the body from fat tissue. It seems that this is a common thing and it's not dangerous, as many people can live with these without any health problems. Later on, I found out that my dad has three of them on his kidneys too.

The blood tests followed and later revealed that I had this parasite, just as he had predicted. I was prescribed antibiotics for two weeks and the nodes disappeared in time. This was the only serious health issue I can remember having over my 22 years of living in Cyprus.

That is why I wasn't worried when the gynaecologist brought up her findings about the kidney lipoma. I have never had any symptoms or problems with my kidneys.

She was happy to hear that I was aware of it and had been diagnosed with this for many years without any health implications. But she was already holding a reference letter addressed to the NHS urology team to investigate this further. I was beginning to feel deeply tired of tests and hospital appointments, but I figured I'd let them know the story, have a test to confirm it was a benign growth and then move on. I wasn't worried about this at all. I was just happy and relieved that the results for the ovarian cysts and blood tests were favourable.

When I left, I felt blessed. Breathing the air that day made me feel free and fresh like never before. I felt like I was appreciating life a tiny bit more than the day before. I guess the big weight had been lifted and that is why I was feeling that way. I remember meeting my sister afterwards for lunch and being so grateful for that time we could spend together.

It's amazing how much your perspective of life can change when you are faced with such situations. We appreciate the little things more. We realize that we are fragile. We remember to cherish the most precious gift we are given when we come into this world. Our body and our health.

I felt just like the willow tree after a strong wind that had turned out to be a false alarm. I could just flow effortlessly with the air as the sun was shining through the branches again.

April 2019

It wasn't mentally easy to keep the business and myself running smoothly, while at the same time I had these health issues to deal with in the background. I was just waiting to hear from them about the next course of action.

Before I knew it, Easter arrived. My sister suggested that we take a car and get away from London for a long weekend. The problem was that the migraines came back. This time, they were more intense than I could ever remember.

We agreed to take a few days off for the Easter holiday. We drove to the Isle of Wight with my sister and three other friends. I was feeling drowsy through the whole journey in the car. I had suffered from motion sickness before, so I thought that was the reason.

By the time we had arrived to the place that we were staying that night, I wasn't feeling well. I couldn't join them for dinner and went straight to bed. The next day I felt better and was looking forward to exploring the place since I'd never been there before. On the ferry, I began to feel a bit drowsy again, but it wasn't too bad.

We got off and went for a walk to sightsee around Totland Bay and Alum Bay. It was all breathtaking and amazingly beautiful. But the migraines came back and were getting worse and worse by the minute. I remember at some point I had to sit down on the grass, as I could not take another step. It seemed that movement made if feel worse.

I sat down on the side of the road to take a small break, feeling as though my head was shaking on the inside. I thought that if I sat down for a bit to rest, it would get better and I could maybe get back up and continue again. This time the pain was like nothing I had felt before. I felt like my head was going to explode.

In the past, whenever I had a headache, I would stay home, and remain isolated without moving or causing it to get worse. Now I was away from home and couldn't do it. I also wanted to enjoy this trip, the beauty of nature and explore that corner of the world. I felt so useless, as I couldn't do anything about it. My body was just refusing to move.

Just when I thought I was past the worst, I started vomiting too. Again, I've rarely ever vomited before. I could only remember it happening two or three times in my whole life, and one of those had been when I had eaten an outdated yoghurt without checking the date first. Even when pregnant, it never happened.

In the car, as we were driving back to the place we were staying, I kept thinking "please don't throw up, please don't throw up…" I could not wait to get out of the car. The moment we arrived there and I stepped foot on the ground, I started projectile vomiting repeatedly. It was really bad, a very scary place. A place I had never found myself before, which was a real nightmare. At the same time, I was feeling terrible about ruining my friends' holiday. Of course, they didn't mind, but they were worried about me and that is exactly what I didn't want.

When we returned to London, my sister drove me straight to the A&E at Saint Thomas' Hospital. We sat down and explained everything in detail: describing the symptoms and how I experienced intense head-aches recurring over a few months. By that time, I was feeling better. The headaches and vomiting were gone.

They examined me using practical neurological tests and I passed all of them. The blood tests showed all was normal. They gave me some painkillers and sent me home. By the time I arrived home, I felt better. I kept thinking I had to get rid of the cysts, as they must be causing me these symptoms. This was by far the worst experience I'd had to that day when it comes to my health.

May 2019

I went to see a GP for the migraines and went into great detail to explain that this pain was so intense that was disrupting not just my health and wellbeing, but also the quality of my life and work as well. I told him how I had to cancel many client sessions over many days while I was suffering from these migraines. He performed similar tests to the ones I'd undergone at the hospital and didn't find anything abnormal.

He continued to argue that the reason for the symptoms could be a premenopausal phase. He prescribed some painkillers, which according to him, would fix everything. He said that, if I took them the moment I started feeling the pain, the pain would not progress and that would be the end of it.

I have never taken regular medication before and I wasn't happy with the idea. He explained that this would only be the case during the days when this headache cycle began. Still, I was not in agreement with ingesting chemicals.

Our body speaks to us through physical symptoms, pleasant or painful. We can tell when something is or isn't right with our health. Pain is the way that our body communicates with us. When we are taking painkillers, it's as if we are telling our body to shut up. We are just numbing the pain, but the problem is still there. Plus, we take painkillers without knowing what is really going on, and we are creating more chemical distress within our body. There was not much I could do at the time, so I decided to wait and see how I felt and if this would happen again.

In the meantime, I was waiting to hear from the NHS about the two health situations. The first thing I was waiting for was the date of the procedure to remove the ovarian cysts. The other, was an appointment to see the urology specialists, clarify the situation and get that off my plate as well.

When a case is not urgent with the NHS it takes more than you can begin to imagine. I had no option but to wait.

It took a while and instead of hearing from the gynecologist first, which was my most burning issue at the time, I received a letter to meet the experts of the urology team about the other issue: the growth in the kidney.

When I went to see the specialist and explained that I had known about this lump and that I had it for years, he thought I was being "very optimistic". Those were his exact words.

Then he kept talking about ways to treat kidney cancer. My face froze listening to him. I could not believe he was trying to have a conversation about that. All I wanted to tell him was, "Wait a minute, I haven't even had the scan yet. Let's do that first and we can cross that bridge when we get there." Instead, I kept my silence and listened. Towards the end, he seemed to have figured out that I didn't need to hear any of that, because just before I left he said, "I'm sure everything will be fine". It's very possible that my facial expressions gave it away.

As I left, I felt very annoyed about the fact that he had the authority to plant seeds in people's minds. I think that is a great responsibility. If I hadn't known for certain that it was just a "fat lump", I would probably have gone mad worrying about it, based on what he had said.

It took a while for me to calm myself, as I was still feeling irritated about his tone and the way he dealt with the situation. I guess it's because I allowed myself to dwell on it too much, thinking of how inappropriate his approach was. However, by the end of the day I felt fine, especially after I talked about it with my son and my sister over the phone.

A few days later, I was notified of an appointment with the surgeon gynaecologist on the 19th of August. That was three months away. I wasn't happy to be honest; I had been expecting something sooner.

I could not go through all that waiting for another three months. What concerned me mostly, was that there was no word about a final date for the surgery. It seemed that this was just an assessment to establish my eligibility for it.

I had to clarify what this was about, so I sat down and started to make some calls. I wanted to find out when I was going to have the surgery. I needed to plan my work and commitments and clarify what would happen during this appointment.

Emotionally and mentally, it had been hard for me ever since I had found out about it. And then the physical limitations. I could not perform physical activities the same way I had before, or with the same intensity. I was restricted in what I could do fitness wise, as there was a possibility of these cysts bursting, a severe implication for my health. Everything seemed to be so tangled up. This is what I meant about a storm within other storms.

I didn't want to wait so long. I just wanted this done and dealt with, so that I could move on, free of all these burdens.

After much patience while listening to a lot of "on hold music" on the phone, I was informed that the appointment would be an assessment, after which I would be placed on a waiting list for this surgery. When I asked how long the list was, they told me it was "somewhere between six to nine months". Wow!

OK, I had not expected that. This meant I had to wait three months until I was even on the waiting list, plus another six to nine months to get it done. That meant, I was looking at almost a year's wait to get the cysts removed. It clearly wasn't going to happen that year. That could not be. I had to do something about it.

June 2019

I started to look at my options. I realised it was a terrible mistake not having private health insurance earlier. Even if I got a new insurance policy at that time, I would not have been covered for pre-existing conditions.

My other option was to have private surgery. After a lot of research, and with the support of close friends and family, I went to see a private gynaecologist and surgeon and agreed to book the surgery on the 7th of July 2019. That would cost me almost £5k which I could not pay in one go at that time. I decided to apply for a private health care surgery loan in the meantime. I was hoping that the answer would be positive. It had to be. The date was just weeks away.

As I was waiting for all of this to be resolved, I had the kidney scan. I remember entering the centre where the scan was taking place; what a terrible feeling it is when you have to walk into a space that is called "Cancer Centre". Just being around that place makes you have worrying thoughts. I take my hat off to all the people who had to go through this terrifying illness; to me they are the bravest souls. The scan took just 10 minutes so I was out of there quickly.

This was supposed to be followed up by an appointment, where they would discuss the results. Because it was overlapping with the same date for the planned keyhole surgery, I asked them to push it forward. They booked me in, just a few days later, which was a bit too soon, but I could not change it again. It was all they had available, and they wanted me to make it there. Do you see what I mean by this continuous series of entangled situations?

A week or so before my birthday on the 18th of June, I had another migraine episode. I had cancelled all my sessions for the day and went home again. It was bad. I had to stay in bed for three days. I couldn't move, eat or do anything. At the same time, I had an early birthday present from my sister. A weekend getaway trip to Ibiza with her and another family friend.

To be honest, I wasn't sure if I was going to make that one. I remember having been in bed since Wednesday and cancelling all sessions until Friday. I could not move at all, because moving my head or standing, would only make it worse.

On Friday, my son and his fiancée came and took me to the A&E again. Nothing different happened. They just gave me some pills and sent me home after we'd been waiting there for hours. I went to my sister's place to sleep there, with the hope that I could make it to Ibiza the next morning.

When I woke up, I felt better and we did make our way to the airport on Saturday morning, after all. I was happy to be able to get away. And I'm always up for a sunny beach. I wasn't feeling great but I enjoyed my stay there without any recurring migraines.

The sound of the sea, the breeze, the sun kisses were all healing elements, and being there was a break that was much needed. I remember I was careful and didn't spend much time under the direct light of the sun. I was feeling weaker and not my usual self the first day. I mostly stayed under the umbrella by the beach.

The change of environment from a busy city to a calm sunny place and the nutritious food made a great difference. It felt like a big breath of fresh air, after you've been locked in a room for days. It was so necessary at that time in my life. When we came back to London, I felt a bit more energised, but still not very strong.

About that time, my house lease was coming to an end and I could not wait to get out of there. I remember looking for a new place, potentially with a flatmate. I loved the area, and I wanted something around there. I was constantly researching but couldn't find anything. As if what I was dealing with wasn't enough already!

There was a lovely walk on my everyday way to the city, and I was observing the flats by the water, wishing that I'd be so lucky as to find a spot like that. Nothing seemed to be available. I wanted to move before the surgery in July and have a fresh start there. Every evening when I sat quietly alone, I dreamt of that.

In the meantime, I received some good news. The surgery loan was approved. A dear friend helped me with that process and I am so grateful to her for that. I finally felt like something started to shift. "That's great I thought to myself, one out of the way!"

A few days went by and just when I had almost lost hope about finding a new place in time, I opened my notifications and found an advert for a flat share with one person not far from where I was. I opened the images and it all seemed so familiar. When I looked closer I've realised, "wait this is just around the corner, I know this view so well". It was just by the water where I used to look at the flats, wishing that I lived there. It came up just like a mushroom out of nowhere.

I said to myself; "this is too much of a coincidence. It has to be it!" I dropped a message to the advertiser and she replied immediately. I went to see the place the next day and loved it, but most importantly, there was something about the girl that felt familiar and lovely. We clicked.

I moved in just two days before the surgery and felt so lucky and blessed to have found this place and this lovely girl. I finally felt like things were coming together for me. The loan was approved, I had found the perfect place for a new home to live in just in time for the surgery; everything was beginning to align again. I moved in on a Friday, settled all my stuff and then on Monday I had the surgery.

July 2019

No one is excited about having surgery, but I was the exception. I could not wait to get this done and wasn't afraid at all. I trusted the surgeon that I had chosen for this and felt safe. She came and saw me as I was getting ready and she explained exactly how and what she was going to be doing during the procedure. I remember her saying that if my ovary was severely damaged due to the big size of the cyst, then she would remove it as well.

Then she reassured me that even if I wanted to have kids again, I would be fine with one ovary. I gave her my approval to go ahead and do whatever she considered was best in my case. And so she did. My right ovary was crushed and she removed it during surgery.

When she came to see me after I woke up from all the "cocktails" she told my sister, who was by my side, "she's as good as gold". I felt lighter that the surgery went well, and happy when my son came to take me home the next day.

A few days later, I had to attend the follow up about the kidney scan at the urology department. I was fresh from the surgery but they insisted I'd go. My sister came with me. We took a cab and went there.

I still remember the doctor that saw me. He read the report and suggested that according to the radiologist, it appeared that the lump was cancerous; then he went on about how this radiologist was one of the best and never missed a scan.

He explained that even if he had to remove one of my kidneys, I would still function properly because my kidney function was 97%, which is great. He was making it sound like nothing.

I could hear what he was saying but none of it could stick. It almost sounded like a joke. It just didn't make sense, simply because I knew deep down that there had to be a mistake. My sister was there with me and she was asking the questions, as she figured out that I wasn't quite following. There was only one question that came to my mind and I asked in the end.

"How can we find out for sure if this is what you think it is?" He suggested a biopsy. For that, I would have to go to the hospital for half a day where they would literally stab my kidney to take a sample and test it, in simple terms.

I wasn't keen to do that, but I agreed to it, even though I did not want to believe in the possibility of having cancer. I most certainly wasn't looking for another hospital experience, especially after the recent surgery. In the end, we agreed it was best to make sure rather than risk it.

My whole existence was focused on fighting to stay strong during the new storm that seemed like it was beginning to unfold. I wasn't even sure if this cold breeze was another false alarm. I truly wanted to believe that. I almost did not want to go ahead with it, but the wisdom of the willow tree softly whispered *"Stay flexible, the truth cannot be hidden"*.

One more time, I made peace with that. Fast forward a few days, and I was being admitted for this procedure.

What I am about to describe in the following paragraphs is one of the things that happens maybe once in a lifetime. Some people call it luck, some call it chance; I call it a miracle. As you read this book, you will see that I have been blessed with this kind of experiences many times.

I remember when they brought me the paperwork and they verbally went through all the risks associated with this procedure, I almost wanted to leave and cancel the whole thing. There were things like the risk of puncturing your gut, liver, internal bleeding, severe internal damage, infections and so many others.

I really didn't want to do this unless it was strictly necessary, so I started to ask a few questions about the procedure, to which they replied that the risks were very low and so on. I remember silently praying and asking the divine energies to give them light and see the truth about my health. I deeply felt that the diagnosis from the last scan was wrong. I just could not get that out of my head, but mostly I felt it in my gut and I knew it in my body. It's almost like my kidney was screaming "Please don't bother me, I have never bothered you".

The nurses came to assess me and helped me get ready for the procedure; they had me wearing a hospital robe and socks. After a long wait I finally got called to the scan room where the operation would take place.

They asked me to lie on the bed, facing down under the CT scan where they would take a few pictures first. The hospital staff were very kind and helpful. The doctor that was assigned to my case came and explained that he would have another colleague assist him with this procedure, a pathological radiologist. Thus, there were two experts allocated to the case.

As I was lying facing down with my lower back exposed ready for the scan pictures, my whole existence was mumbling silently, "please give them light, please give them light". Once the scan pictures were taken, they told me that it was over so I could relax a bit while they take a look at them.

They all went into the next room with all the monitors, and there followed a short period of silence. Next, I could hear them muttering something, but could not understand what they were saying. I wished I could hear better. As if someone had heard my request, the nurse sitting at the door waiting for their instructions started to walk up and down. I knew something was up and started to stare at her. Next thing, she came over and said, "Relax, this is not going to happen". My heart suddenly started to pump faster with excitement and confusion at the same time.

Then the pathological radiologist came out to talk to me. He introduced himself; from the name I figured that he was Greek. I was glad to hear that and I started to exchange a few words in Greek. He seemed glad and surprised to hear that I could speak his native language.

He asked me to brief him about when and how I had first found out that I had this lump. And so, I told him the whole story. Again. Then he explained that it was indeed a fat lump and that if we pierced this kind of tissue it might start to bleed uncontrollably and they didn't want to do that. I could not believe it! I was so happy and relieved to hear what he was saying. I felt like my prayers had been magically answered. I opened up about it and told him how I had felt about the diagnosis and that I believed it was not a correct reading. For that reason, I wouldn't want to put myself in any danger unless this was really necessary.

He pulled over an ultrasound machine and had another look through that as well just to confirm that the lump was indeed a lipoma. He was convinced. He finally concluded; "We are not doing this today and we will repeat the test by doing an MRI just to make sure, before we rush to do anything". You can't imagine the thrill I felt. I was living a miracle. I was repeating silently, "I knew it, I knew it, I knew it in my gut…thank you, thank you, thank you".

We tend to describe miracles as something extraordinary. Something beyond our expectations, and outside ourselves. Now, I know that miracles begin with accepting and believing the possibility that we deserve miracles. We all have the power to create miracles when we break through the walls of limitation and connect with something divine that lies both within and beyond our human nature. I always had this belief that *anything is possible*. And I still know it is.

He asked me to go back and put on my clothes, then he would come back to confirm the way forward. Cancelling such a protocol with the NHS is not an easy thing to do, especially when it's a case that they have classified as highly urgent.

I got up and walked away from that room, speechless at what had just happened. I felt so humble and grateful for this miracle. I truly believe that the universe puts the right people at the right time in your life experiences. This could have ended in a very bad way, if it wasn't for this doctor who had the knowledge and light that he did at the time. I remembered the willow's whisper of wisdom: *"The truth will come to light"*. I will never forget this experience. How could I ever?

I went back to my bed, got dressed, excited and happy that I was being spared this. He came by after he had a chat with the team from the other hospital. This was the team that had sent me there in the first place. It was hard for him to convince them of his findings and conclusion. They had insisted that I redo this procedure at another time and stay an extra day in the hospital if needed.

When he related it to me, I felt like I was just an experiment. They knew that the consequence of having my kidney pierced could result in severe bleeding and they still insisted on offering me an extra day in the hospital. I agreed to a date just so that I could get him off the hook, but in the meantime, I organised a follow up, which was booked a long way in advance. This was supposed to be the follow up to discuss the biopsy, but since that did not happen, I kept my appointment anyway with the aim of clarifying this once and for all.

I felt frustrated that I had to go through this without it being necessary. It felt like I was being compelled to do something just to meet the procedures so that the case can be closed. At the same time, I understood that their aim was to identify any serious health issues in good time and deal with them and that my case was on their urgent priority list; however, it wasn't necessary for me to go through that emotional rollercoaster just to be ticked off a list.

On the positive side of things, my recovery after the keyhole surgery for the removal of the ovarian cysts, went very well and three weeks later I was back in business feeling better and stronger than ever before.

August 2019

I was so looking forward to ending this whole misinterpreted diagnosis and to getting on with my life. When I went to the follow up appointment, this other specialist seemed more relaxed and understanding. I explained the whole story, AGAIN, from the beginning including the latest events. I clarified that I did not want them to stab my kidney unless it was absolutely necessary. He recorded everything and agreed with everything I said. He even apologised for the emotional stress I had to go through.

We looked at the scan and he was also in agreement that it did indeed seem like a lipoma. I requested another MRI to put this story behind us and stop all this going back and forth.

A couple of weeks later, after another scan and more waiting, they confirmed that it was not cancerous. That was something I already knew. I did feel very frustrated about the whole thing. It made be doubt many things about the whole system, for many reasons which I may decide to share in the future. On the other hand, I was so glad that it was over. It hadn't been a storm after all, just a short torrential rain shower.

September 2019

Just when things seemed like they were heading the right way, another moon cycle was completed and the headaches came back again. I was so disappointed because I really thought that the cysts had been causing all of that. Clearly there was something else. I took some of the medication prescribed to me, but it didn't make it go away completely. It wasn't as aggressive as the other times, but it was still there. I began to worry about my clients' sessions and had to plan everything around it again. Up to this point with all that had happened, my business had been adversely affected, and my financial situation wasn't great at all, while bills were coming in as usual.

I remember one time when I started to think that this had to be about more than just my cycle. I was going back home after a long day and I was carrying my bag on my right shoulder. It was a bit heavy. As I got off the bus after crossing the road, it felt like I lost my balance on my right side and began to feel weak in the left knee; after taking a few more steps, I ended up on one knee on the ground and someone helped me up. I had no headache at the time, but was on my cycle so I thought it might be something to do with the combination of that and the hot weather. However, that was the first moment that got me thinking. I sat down on a bench for a minute and then I felt just fine, so I continued to walk home.

After all these false alarms, storms and emotional experiences on top of a busy schedule, I truly felt exhausted: mentally and emotionally drained. From the beginning of the year, there were so many things going on around my health. The chickenpox, the migraines, the ovarian cysts, the surgery, the kidney scans, the waiting, the biopsy that didn't happen, more scans and more results...

It's not easy to keep yourself together, especially when you work in an environment where people look up to you for inspiration. It was my job to keep people motivated and healthy and show positivity every day in spite of all that was going on behind the scenes. It all felt like I could not hold any more balls up in the air and I really needed a break to fill my glass. For the last few months I kept saying to myself, once this is behind me, I'm going to take a break and lie down on a sunny beach.

Changing environment, means changing energy. So, I decided on a quick getaway and went to Cyprus where my two dear friends were waiting for me. It was so lovely to finally be able to relax and feel a complete change of environment so I could recharge and start again.

Being back in a place where I'd spent 22 years of my life and made a lifetime worth of friends and family always gave me a positive feeling, as if I was back home. Add to that being by the beach, hearing the sound of the waves, eating delicious Greek fresh food and being away from the city rhythms and pollution; it all recharged me in so many ways and yes, it did fill my empty glass.

Even though it was just for a few days, it was perfect. Little did I know how much I needed this as preparation for what was coming. I hope you are buckled up by now. If you're not, please fasten your seat-belts.

October 2019

I arrived back to London feeling happy and recharged, ready for a fresh start and full of business ideas and plans. I was thinking how I could make up for the downturn I had been experiencing up to that point of the year. I bet you can now understand how I became one of those people who could not wait for that year to come to an end.

Sadly, my renewed energy didn't last for long. Two weeks after I got back from Cyprus, I caught a cold. I couldn't remember the last time I had one. I think it must have been years; it rarely happens to me. That day I went to work, but by lunch time I felt so ill and my nose started to run constantly. I cancelled all remaining sessions and went back home. My flatmate was a bit worried when she saw me returning early, but I told her I had a cold and needed to get some soup and some sleep.

I felt weak. I remember ordering soup online. I just wanted some ready-made food, as I was too fragile to stand and prepare anything on my own. When the delivery came, I heard the buzz for the main entrance. I got out of bed to press the intercom to let him in. He was then supposed to come upstairs, knock on my door and hand over the delivery. But, I remember getting up from my bed and checking with my flatmate; "You know that delivery guy rang the door downstairs but he never came upstairs to bring the soup". And she replied, "I heard you open the door and someone gave you something and then left. I think you've put it in the kitchen."

I went to the kitchen and, to my big surprise, saw that the soup was there on the table still in the delivery bag. That was the second time I noticed that something was wrong, but the first time I realised something was seriously off with me. I could not remember anything from the moment I had pressed the button to open the door downstairs until the moment I asked my flatmate about the soup. All the information in between was missing from my short-term memory. I was too weak and my mind was too blurry to do anything, so I went to bed again and fell asleep.

The next day I was still in bed but most of it is a complete blur. It seems everyone, my sister, my son, mom and even my friends and close clients were messaging me, and I was replying but wasn't making much sense. There were many typos and words that did not make sense. I wasn't aware of any of this at the time; only much later.

My sister called to check on me, but I can't remember any of the discussions I had with her that day over the phone. I only remember her showing up at the door, ready to take me to the emergency department again.

They were all in touch and had figured it out that something was terribly wrong with me. This part again it's still a blur, as I don't remember the details and the right sequence of the facts.

The only thing that I remember was, that I arrived at the emergency room at St Thomas's hospital in London for the third time that year.

THE STORM

To this point in my life, I sincerely believed that if a soul had to pay some debts to the universe, I was certain that I'd already overpaid. Astoundingly, I was proved wrong. There was more. Much more. Something I'd never imagined it was possible for me to experience in this lifetime.

I was at the A&E again, going through the same series of medical examinations. It felt like I was stuck in a loop. Only this time, my sister requested and insisted that I have a proper head scan. All of this is still a blur to me. The brain fog at the time made everything seem fuzzy. The MRI scan was completed. I can't remember clearly the moment when they revealed the diagnosis. It's still a very obscured, almost faded memory. Like someone had hit my head with a brick, but then I felt numb and fell into a dream world.

Another huge storm had started out of nowhere and I did not know what was happening to me. I was in the middle of it, but it seemed like I was watching it through a misty glass. The branches of the willow tree were madly blown by the wet, furious wind, hitting my face but I could not feel anything. I wasn't sure if this was real or I was dreaming.

Just like that, out of nowhere, I was diagnosed with a right convexity meningioma: a brain tumour on the right side of the brain, which, for some reason, had begun to bleed. That was the reason I was feeling confused and disoriented and had clearly been the cause of all the severe headaches over the previous seven months.

At that time, I was in a critical condition; as a result, I do not recall the exact moment when they communicated the diagnosis. I try to remember, but I can only place small parts of it. It felt like I was in a trance, and, although a part of me understood that this diagnosis was very serious, I didn't really feel any emotional pain that I can recollect. It was almost as if my soul was numb, or that the conscious part of the brain was not firing up to register this new information and to give it a meaning. Either way, it didn't even matter because it all came back to me in avalanches of emotions two days later.

It's still a huge mystery to me how I'd never had any other symptoms during all that time, until the migraines of the previous few months. It's also strange that they did not consider the scan option, given my records of the migraines and several visits at the emergency. I'm not sure how this would have turned out if my sister didn't insist for that scan.

The neurology team of experts at the Kings College hospital in London were immediately informed and have sent through specific instructions for strong medication to be administered instantly. They also requested that I should be transferred there the next day. I was put on steroids right away to reduce the inflammation and bleeding which was causing the severe headaches and short-term memory loss.

The next 24 hours lying in a bed at St Thomas's Hospital emergency department are all distorted in my head. I can't remember much, if any of it. My recollection of events slowly started to come back the next day in the afternoon, just before the ambulance came to pick me up and transport me to Kings College Hospital.

Funnily, I can only recall how I was complaining to my sister that they were supposed to come at 6 pm and they were 15 minutes late. I think I was conscious enough at the time, to have registered this memory.

At that point, the confusion started to part slowly and I had a bit more clarity. I remember being very chatty in the ambulance and talking to the driver and the assistant nurse. All this time my little sister Paula was with me. She had informed all our family of the terrifying news while I was there overnight. I can only imagine what a shock this must have been for everyone.

She told them to stay home until there was more clarity on what was going to happen after I was moved. On the evening of 10th of October 2019, I was admitted at the neurosurgery department at Kings. It was a Thursday.

After I said goodbye to my sister, I was asked to sit on a wheelchair to my left. A chaperone began to wheel me along the corridors of the hospital. I could see that I was heading towards a big dark room. By that time, the lights were dimmed, to allow the patients to get some rest, I guessed.

The vibe felt so strange, and the place seemed too quiet. It was something of an odd world that I had no idea even existed. I could see there were many patients with neurological issues, and I could not believe it. It's like all this time I had been living in a different world. Finally, the chair stopped rolling and the chaperone showed me to what was going to be my bed for many days ahead.

A male nurse came to help me settle in and to assess me for the upcoming surgery. We went through a very long medical health questionnaire. Once that was done, he handed me a robe and some hospital socks to change. He seemed very nice and reassuring.

Even though I'd never thought that life would see me lying on this hospital bed, there I was and there was nothing I could do to make it go away. I had never liked needles; when he took my blood samples, I closed my eyes and turned my head the other way.

After he left with the samples, I began to notice everything around me. I'd never thought about or knew that there were so many people in similar situations. It looked like they were sleeping; I was wondering what their reasons were for being there.

I noticed the nurse who seemed to be in charge that evening: an Asian man with white hair and big black framed glasses. He looked very familiar and I could not figure out why at the beginning. A bit later, after watching him some more checking on every patient, I noticed that he resembled my brother-in-law from Sweden. Even though my whole existence was partially numb and my body was weak, tired and hungry, a part of me smiled because he felt familiar.

In the middle of the room, there were a couple of beds surrounded by blue curtains to keep their privacy. I could not see who was in there, but after the male nurse went in to check on them, the patient inside started to scream like he was going to be executed. The whole ward could hear his yells. "This place is so creepy," I thought to myself. I wanted to run away.

After a while, everything went quiet again. My mind began to flood with burning questions.

The patient lying in the bed next to mine appeared to be a young man, probably in his twenties. His eyes were closed the whole time; he wasn't moving nor speaking at all. He had some tubes coming out of his nose which were connected to a bag of pink liquid. At the time I had no idea what that was, but later I found out that it was basically liquid food. I couldn't stop wondering; "Does he have something similar to what I have? Why isn't he moving at all? Did the surgery go well; is he okay?"

Then my attention shifted to myself. I couldn't stop thinking and asking myself how I had found myself there. It was surreal that I was lying in a hospital bed with a life-threatening diagnosis. What a nightmare. Sadness took over my soul for a while, to a spell of tears and sorrow. And then more questions followed.

"How did this happen to me? I've always been active and felt strong. I ate healthily most of the time, and regularly hydrated myself. I never smoked and only consumed alcohol occasionally. How could I have contracted such an illness? A brain tumour? Really? I hate this place, I don't want to be here, I want to go home."

Just the thought of it was preposterous. It was extremely hard to grasp that the nightmare was actually reality.

After another cascade of emotions, I felt lighter and wiped off my heavy tears. I could hear my body's whispers of hunger so my attention drifted to my survival instinct. It was no wonder, as I remembered that I had been without food for more than 24 hours by that time. Plus, two hours had passed by and there was no news about the surgery. Finally, around 10 pm the new nurse, a young girl, came and told me that I could eat something that evening after all, as the surgery wasn't going to happen that night. It had been postponed until the next day.

I was very happy to hear that, simply because I was so hungry. I could have eaten just about anything. She brought me an apple, a muffin and some biscuits as it was all that was left in their kitchen. I'd never felt happier to see food before me. I ate everything, and asked for a cup of tea as well, as I still wasn't full; I thought that a warm sip would settle it for me, and it did. I remember sending pictures of myself and the apple to my family on the chat, telling them that I was so excited to finally have some food.

The nurse came back again and gave me a handful of pills to take. Some were to reduce the inflammation and some were to avoid any potential seizures that could have happened overnight.

She told me that I wasn't supposed to eat anything else after the tea, as there was a possibility I would have the operation in the morning. She said I had to be "nil by mouth"; the medical terminology for no food, which is standard before a surgery or similar procedure. I still remember feeling a bit confused. I was obviously still very tender and disorientated. I began to feel drowsy and tired and fell asleep after that.

That same night, I had a really strange experience. As I was sleeping, a voice suddenly woke me up. As I opened my eyes, I thought I saw my brother-in-law. I remember feeling happy to see him. I thanked him for the surprise and I think I may have even hugged him. I remember telling him that it was too late and that he was not supposed to be there at that time. "It's best you come tomorrow," I said to him. Or at least this is what I believe happened.

Then suddenly he wanted to give me something to drink, and literally poured the drink into my mouth. I could not see what it was but I remember spitting it out and fighting him, yelling that I couldn't drink or eat anything as I was going to have my surgery the next day and I wasn't allowed anything by mouth.

He struggled with me a little more and then he left me alone. This is a bit cloudy, but I thought there was also another person with him, someone who was holding my hands while he was trying to pour that liquid into my mouth.

I remember my robe getting wet and my chest feeling cold because of the spilled drink. I thought he had wanted to give me some sort of liqueur. It tasted bitter-sweet. He likes his "distinctive" drinks. After he left my side, I watched him going to all the other beds doing what I thought was pretending to be a doctor checking on the patients. He is naturally humorous and entertaining like that. I wanted to tell him, "Please don't do that. It's not funny. You will get in trouble." He was even talking to them.

I tried to reach for my phone to take a picture of him doing that, and to send it to his wife, my sister. I wanted to tell on him, but my phone was out of reach as it had dropped on the floor during the struggle. I tried a couple of times, but my hand could not get that far down to the floor. I gave up, as I felt too weak to get off the bed, so I fell back asleep.

The next day my family came to visit me. My middle sister, who was living in Sweden, had booked a flight the same night I was admitted to the hospital. The moment she found out, she dropped everything and came to the UK. I was so happy to see her that morning. I asked her if my brother-in-law, her husband, was there as well. I felt confused when she said no. I was convinced that he had come to visit me; I remember trying to explain to her what had happened the night before. Smiling, she said that it was impossible because he was in South Africa on a business trip so there was no way that it could have been him.

It all seemed very confusing to me, and I was so puzzled. I had been sure it was him. Then I thought I must have been dreaming, until I had finally figured out what had really happened.

The next day, the Asian male nurse told me that they had come to my bed the night before and tried to do some sort of test to see my reaction. It hadn't been my brother-in-law that tried to have me drink whatever that liquid was, but the Asian male nurse that looked just like him in my mind. I realised that my serious condition at that time, coupled with the drugs, had caused me to have some form of hallucination while I was half asleep.

It's crazy what a movie our brain can play when influenced by chemicals. It is so believable. Hallucinations are a real thing and the fascinating part, is that the brain uses bits of information which come from real evidence that we collect in our memory. Then it uses that info and gets into role-play, creating a whole new movie.

In my case, the resemblance was real. The fact that they had come by to check on me and to give me some medication was real too. The fact that my brother-in-law is comical and he likes his drinks is also a fact. The rest was just a montage between facts and imagination.

I'm still not sure why they did what they did, but I know that the next day, when the doctor on call was doing his rounds on the ward to check on each patient, he came by my bed and said, "You look great. You will get your own private room today." And that very day, they moved me to a private room all by myself. It seemed they'd finally understood that I didn't belong in the dark, creepy room anymore, where people scream when the night falls.

As I was waiting to be moved to the new room, I noticed that the young guy with the tubes just across my bed had visitors. I was pleased to see that. It looked like the visitor was his dad, and he was talking to him, even though he did not seem to be responding much. It must have been so hard for his family to see him like that. I mean it was hard enough for me, a stranger to him.

Later that day, I moved to a new private room and everything began to be clearer. This was only because the mental confusion caused by the inflammation of the growth had started to clear out. The chemicals and the steroids were clearly effective, and that helped me to better understand with more clarity what my was condition at that time.

An expert from the neurosurgery team came to see me and explained in great detail the diagnosis and the exact state I was in. That's when I was informed that the tumour was in the superficial layers in between the skull and not the actual brain tissue. This is why it had been diagnosed as a meningioma. The bleeding and swelling of the brain had been affecting my short-term memory for the 48 hours before admission. It seemed that it was a very slow growth, that must have developed there over the period of ten years, they concluded. It had reached the huge size of approximately 11 cm, he said. I was astounded again.

He told me how the surgery was planned to unfold. There was so much information, and while I understood what he was saying, a part of me wanted to believe it was just a nightmare and I'd wake up from it soon.

It became very real when we started to go through the paperwork I had to sign for them to go ahead with everything that he had just described. There was a huge list of the many risks and things that could go wrong during and after the surgery. To say the least, there was the risk of infection, stroke, and even death. I wasn't in a place where I could negotiate anything. I had no choice so I signed it off, of course.

This was around three days after I had been admitted when I was still waiting for my turn. My family was also going through a very hard time, and the wait achieved nothing but to increase the level of their worry and anxiety.

I can't say that I was looking forward to having my skull opened, but I wanted to know when I was going to have the procedure. The wait was getting longer and longer, but they couldn't give me an exact date for the surgery. They explained that they were very busy with extremely urgent life and death cases that were coming in all the time. Since all my vitals seemed to be doing well, I wasn't considered to be in "immediate danger".

They clarified that it was also best to monitor and reduce the inflammation as much as possible before going ahead with the surgery. It seemed that the drugs were working. Those steroids made me so hungry. I had an incredible appetite for food all the time. I was eating anything and everything. I was craving foods that had never been in my diet, like ketchup. I had rarely even touched that, as I just don't like it. I know! I'm one of these weirdos. I remember when my nephew and my son saw me eating ketchup and fries, they were really surprised and started to laugh with me.

Other than consuming large amount of foods every day, there was nothing I could do but wait until the right time and feel grateful that at least I wasn't considered a matter of extreme urgency. There were other people that needed surgery more than myself at that time.

Needless to say, that I was closely monitored day and night. My blood pressure, body temperature and regular blood tests were taken all the time and reported to the neurosurgeons. The worst was during the night, when the nurses would wake me up every three or four hours to do that.

By this time, my sister had informed all our close friends about the sudden diagnosis and that I had been hospitalised and was waiting to receive surgery. They were devastated. I can't even imagine how hard it must have been, firstly for my sister to tell them, and then for them to hear it.

My phone was packed with hundreds of messages and missed calls that had been coming through over the previous three days. I did not have the mental or emotional strength to deal with any of them at that time.

Most of my friends who knew my sister were briefed, but not everyone knew exactly what was going on. They all wanted to find out what was happening, as many of them didn't exactly know. To be honest, it was very hard to deal with that. In between the visits of my family and dear close friends, I would grab my phone but I just did not know how to start. My heart was broken and I did not want to break theirs too.

How do you tell someone that your life has been put on hold? How do you tell them that you are petrified and you have no idea what has hit you and where it came from? How do you find the words to tell your clients, friends, and coworkers that you have been diagnosed with a tumor, you are going to have brain surgery and you have no idea what will happen after?

I did respond to some of the messages and calls, but I could not possibly manage all of them. I handed the phone to my sister and she took over, replying to everyone and explaining the situation. I am still astounded by the strength she had to deal with all of this.

I felt so blessed to have had the support of my family and close friends. They were by my side all this time. They were visiting every day and were there for me, bringing me food, drinks and spoiling me with anything I needed. Needless to say, they were all surprised by the appetite and positivity I was showing. It was probably partially because of all the drugs and the steroids.

At night when I was alone lying on that hospital bed, when no one could see or hear me, cascades of burning tears were sliding down my cheeks. I still could not believe what was happening. The load was way beyond anything else before. It felt like something I would never be able to carry. I felt like I had been through so much in my life already, and had thought I was done with the hardships. I had no idea where I would find the strength to make it through this one. I guess I was trying to find something to hold on to and pull myself up.

My soul was trembling with fear and sorrow as I remembered that my uncle had died when I was 14, after having a brain tumour removed. He had only been 23. It was so painful to lose him that way. It never crossed my mind that I would ever face this illness as well. Yet it was real.

At the same time, I couldn't begin to imagine what was happening in the hearts of my loved ones. What a chaos this must have caused. I knew I had to stay strong and deal with my own physical and emotional pain, but my heart was going out to my family and I was thinking about the terror this must have caused in their hearts and lives. I mean, my parents were miles and miles away. I could just feel their pain and imagine how heart-breaking it was for them. I never wanted to cause them any suffering.

I was also feeling gutted about my business; my clients, classes, the journey we'd started together, their goals and their plans and everything we had been looking forward to together. Everything was just falling apart. I felt like I'd let them down and at the same time I was watching everything I had worked for slipping through my fingers like grains of sand.

There were phases when I was trying to find someone to blame. The fact that it wasn't detected earlier, despite the fact that medical personnel are trained to identify these things, seemed like the perfect place to start. It was just unacceptable. "How come they haven't thought of taking this scan before? How is it possible that after so many visits at the hospital and GP, they didn't figure it out sooner?

Then I started to blame myself. "I should have taken better care of myself and looked into this issue more..."

When I got tired of all the blaming, I realised that it didn't change the situation in any way. Even if this had been picked up earlier, it wouldn't have changed the fact that I had it. However, the reality that it wasn't picked up despite the repetitive visits at the hospital, was still playing on my mind, and so I decided that one day, I wanted to raise this issue, not to look for justice, but to raise awareness so that this wouldn't happen to anyone else. The more I thought about it, the more I understood that I was very lucky to be alive.

It was very frightening for me to remember that, while I had a brain tumour, not to mention of that size, I had undergone a keyhole surgery and been under anaesthetic for almost two hours to remove the ovarian cysts back in July.

Then I'd magically escaped from being pierced in my kidney due to a misinterpreted scan after that surgery.

It was even scarier to remember what I had been through back in April, when I had projectile vomiting and nausea while I was trying to enjoy Easter away from home. I simply couldn't believe how my body had bounced back so quickly after such internal chaos.

I also remembered that I had actually got on an aeroplane and flown back and forth two times. One of those times, I had been by myself. All this had been just a few months before I was diagnosed, while my brain was silently bleeding. Thinking about this just blew my mind. Can you even begin to imagine how wrong things could have gone? I could have easily just fallen down somewhere or had a seizure or heaven knows what else, while no one had any idea what was truly going on.

Reflecting on all this made me realise with great humility how blessed and lucky I was to still be there, in one piece. Some people call this fortune. For me, as you know by now, the perfect word is miracle. I recognised that, to be there in that moment, after everything that has happened throughout the year, was a major life phenomenon. In fact, it was the result of a series of miracles. What a blessing it was to have this revelation.

When the tears dried out, I began to feel like the clouds started to slowly part again and that, somehow, they took all the pain and heavy emotions with them.

I felt lighter and I noticed how I could breathe more easily. It was as if the sky had cleared after a torrential rainstorm. With a bit more clarity of thought, I asked myself, "Right, so what now? How do I move on? What is my next step? Can I even take a step right now?"

I understood that the only way to make it through this storm was firstly to accept that there was really no one to blame.

The next thought that came to me, was that none of us can ever be prepared for something like this; but that doesn't mean that if it does happen, we should give up on life. There will be all sort of experiences, some more pleasant than other, but that doesn't mean we should turn away from them. It's still part of your life experience. All life is to be honoured.

Just like when a bee stings you, it happens fast, you have no time to react and avoid it. You feel numb, confused and in pain for a while. But then you bring yourself together and find a way to get up and move on.

After taking that inner dive, I promised myself that I was going to take this experience day by day, breath by breath and step by step. It was the only way. I knew that I could not fight it, nor change it. I knew I had to allow it to unfold. And that was very difficult.

I guess the hardest thing for me, was to let go of everything that I had built so far, and all the plans I had made for my future and for my business; everything that I had been trying to hold on to, including the self-image that I had been trying to protect and maintain. I had to reach great depths within myself to find the strength I needed, to let go of everything I had known. Then, I knew I needed to surrender to the current of the flow. And in order to surrender we only need one thing. Trust.

When the strong winds blow, the willow tree joins the dance, step by step and movement by moment, until the storm is over. It doesn't resist it nor refuse it, but honours the role it plays in the grand order of nature. It does not fear surrender because it trusts mother nature.

To be completely honest, I wasn't exactly sure how I was going to navigate this experience and see it all the way through, but the one-day-at-a-time approach seemed to have hit home for me. I decided to keep my calm and trust the greater intelligence that had been by my side through the many storms in my life. It was that same intelligence that had kept me safe when things could have gone terribly wrong.

Despite all the challenges I'd lived through, I could not stop thinking how I had always felt the love of the universe through people, situations, synchronicities and the grace that had helped me make it through each time. I knew that with every storm there is a blessing. And I say this, because even though it's always a rough ride, we are given all the tools we need to make it through.

Now, once again, I found myself in the middle of a storm. Even though it was overwhelming, like nothing I have ever experienced before, the biggest part of me felt like I had so much to be thankful for.

In fact, I had everything to be grateful for. I was equipped with the greatest arsenal anyone could have. Full family support and wonderful friends. What else do you need in times like that? When you feel the warmth of the hands of your family members and friends holding yours, you can go to the end of the world and make anything happen. It was such a reassuring and comforting feeling to have them by my side.

I felt so grateful that God had offered me a big hand of support, not only through the love of my family and friends, but also through some perfect orchestrations such as being in the perfect place at the right time. I was under the care and supervision of the most experienced team in the neurosurgery arena in London; people who were top in their field. They knew exactly what they were doing and were planning every detail for my case. I had everything to be grateful for indeed.

I was beginning to feel positive. I could feel the vibrations of trust and faith again through my body. Yes, I was ready to take this on. I could see a tiny light at the end of the tunnel and I had hope that I will make my way there.

REBIRTH

On the 18th of October, after eight days of regular medication, continuous monitoring, countless needles piercing my veins, bruises and sleepless nights, the day of the surgery finally arrived. The surgery team was prepared to take me to the theatre for the operation.

I was ready and all prayed up, and as they began to wheel and manoeuvre my bed through the corridors of the hospital on the way down to the theatre, I felt my heart starting to beat rapidly. My sisters were there, holding my hands, one on the left and one on the right. I was feeling a bit anxious, but I smiled and told them that I was happy to be finally getting this done. We had all been waiting for this long enough. Just before entering the lift, we separated and I said to them "See you later".

The bed stopped a level down, in front of the theatre, where I met the anaesthetist and the assistant surgeon. It was around eleven o'clock in the morning. The lead surgeon wasn't there yet. We started chatting and went through some paperwork again. He was making conversation and asking me about the source of my Greek surname. I told him the story. This unfolded just outside the operating room.

The theatre door was quite narrow; it didn't seem wide enough for the bed to go through. I offered to walk in myself, if needed. They were happy with that, and so I stepped into the theatre. In that instant, I felt as if I had walked into a fridge. It was so cold in there. Extremely cold. The room was empty. I could barely see anything, apart from some apparatus in the middle of the room. The anaesthetist followed me in. For some strange reason, I wasn't feeling fearful. Maybe it was because I was feeling so cold at that moment. Or it could have been because I almost heard the willow tree whispering: *"You're safe, surrender to the moment. It will be all right."*

He asked me to lie down on something that looked like a tall flat bench. It was quite narrow. As I laid down, I could see a screen displaying a humanoid head, coming down from the sealing. I've never seen anything like that in real life, just in movies. I figured, that was the guide they were using for the operation. He kept talking, but I can't remember anything else after that. This is about the last thing I remember. I was out before they started to prepare me for the operation, which included shaving a part of my head.

When you find yourself lying on a hospital bed waiting to have surgery, especially brain surgery, I guess it would be natural to have thoughts like, "What if I don't make it after this". The crazy thing? That thought may have crossed my mind, but it didn't stay for too long. It passed through. Maybe I was naive or optimistic, but while I had been waiting for that day to come, I had gone over many things in my head. I had thought of how I'd style my hair after the surgery and how this procedure could affect the quality of my life forever, but the thought of dying didn't stick to me. At least not at that time.

On the other side, my family did not know what to expect. The doctors told them that anything could happen. My case was quite rare. It was of the biggest tumour they had seen that hadn't been causing symptoms like seizures or other complications. Usually, when it gets to a size around 4cm, people start to develop different symptoms, like loss of hearing, nausea, numbness in the limbs and, most commonly, seizures. In my case, it was three times that size and I had experienced nothing like that, apart from the migraines and last-minute memory loss. However, the bigger the tumour, the more "surprises" it can bring they say.

I wasn't aware of this fact, until much later after the surgery, but my family wasn't actually promised anything. The doctors weren't sure if this was going to be a successful operation. They did not exclude the possibility of me having motor function issues, like not being able to speak, or walk or move at all. Nothing was guaranteed.

Much later along, my little sister had confessed about the struggle of the waiting game that all my family had gone through during the eight hours that I was undergoing surgery. When they called the hospital to ask about the status of the operation, and the nurse said, "She is out and in the recovery room," they were just so relieved and happy that I was alive. They could finally breathe with more ease, she said.

In the meantime, on my side, I was starting to feel my awareness gradually returning. It felt like I was coming out of a deep sleep, but I could barely open my eyes. I tried to, but they seemed so heavy and impossible to fully open. I managed to open them a crack, and a tiny thread of light came through my eyelashes. In the background, I was hearing noises and people chatter, but I could not recognise them. My body was feeling very weak and all my senses were confused. I could not remember where I was. In a flash, I thought I was somewhere in a room at the club where I used to work out. It's funny to now realise that the place I thought I was in, it's literally called Third Space. As in "third dimension". How bizarre!

I could hear a constant bleeping. My head was aching and I could not move my body; it felt very heavy. As my awareness was slowly making its way back in, the sounds around me began to be sharper and clearer by the minute. I could hear a voice calling something. I knew it was my name. The next moment, I figured that the bleeping was the sound of my heart beating fast through the heart monitor. My cognition was slowly coming back.

The voice was the nurse constantly talking to me. She was calling my name and telling me that I had just had brain surgery and was in the recovery room. I was trying so hard to open my eyes, but I could only do it for couple of seconds and then had to close them.

She kept talking to me constantly, as she wanted to bring me fully back to being conscious. She started to ask me details, like my name, if I knew where I was and if I could understand what she was talking about. I mumbled a "Yes". Everything was so blurry in my mind, it was hard to articulate words, but I responded because I remembered what had happened, who I was and where I was. I was just feeling too weak to have a conversation; but it was a good sign. Some people can't respond or remember details after brain surgery. I remember her also saying something about me having had a 40 seconds seizure just before I was coming out of the anaesthesia. She was lovely as she explained everything patiently. All came back to me and I remembered the last details before everything had gone dark.

When she was convinced that I was stable enough, she explained that we had to perform an MRI scan as the experts wanted to see what my head looked like on the inside after the operation.

I could not move an inch of my body at that time and so they manoeuvred me throughout the whole process of the MRI scan. I remember they laid me flat and placed my head into a metal support so that I couldn't move it at all.

The scan was performed, and half an hour later, I was taken back upstairs to a new ward on a different floor. As she was pushing my bed down the corridors, she explained that I was being moved to another ward and that all my stuff was also being brought upstairs. I was taken to the third floor, Bed 17.

My vision was blurred and voice was very weak, but I was happy to see my sister and son walking in just minutes after. They had not been allowed in all together, just a couple at the time.

I remember one of my sisters asked me something in English while she was capturing the moment on her phone. Then she asked me something in Romanian as well. I understood both languages and I murmured something about being happy to be alive and that I love my family.

They only stayed for a couple of minutes. The nurses asked them to allow me to get some rest, as I was fresh from the surgery and needed plenty of sleep. By that time, it was already around 8 pm.

The fact that I could speak both languages, and had a normal short conversation was a great sign that the surgery had gone well and nothing else was affected. I felt very tired even just speaking a few words. But what a miracle... I was back. Reborn. The surgery had been successful.

The 24 hours after the operation were serious. They were monitoring me every 15 minutes and then every half hour and then every hour and so on. The first night was considered to be critical. I was well despite everything, and I could hear what was going on around me, but I felt very weak. I had oxygen tubes in my nose, cannulas in my veins to give me infusions and a drain attached to my brain to allow any excessive blood to drain outside of the skull. It was pretty heavy altogether. But my heart was beating, and I was happy to be there realising that I had actually made it through the belly of the dragon.

The first night after the surgery was blurry; I was mostly sleeping in between the frequent monitoring and medication I was given. The staff were so lovely and kind, very caring people. I remember they were constantly asking me if I was in pain or if I needed anything at all. I took some painkillers that night to help me get some rest.

The next day I recall opening my eyes and waking up feeling very hungry. Breakfast round came quickly and I had some toast, jam and tea. That was just to keep me until my son and his fiancée came by; they brought me some delicious home-made food that my sisters had cooked for me. I was so happy to see them and I knew they were happy to see me alive and eating too. My jaw was sore, but that did not stop me. I enjoyed my food very slowly.

The hospital had a decent kitchen and food that was prepared daily for all patients, but I always preferred home-made food over eating out and my family knew that. They also knew that I was quite fussy with nutrition, so they were making sure I was spoiled.

My right eye and right cheek were a dark purple colour in the morning and, in the afternoon, it got quite swollen as well. When I saw myself on my phone camera, I smiled, as I resembled a little boy with a white turban and a bulldog eye. It made me giggle when I noticed that I could not see over my right cheek when I was looking down. That first morning after the surgery, the experts had come to visit me and confirmed that they had removed the whole tumour and that everything looked great in the scan I had just after the surgery. I felt extremely happy hearing that. My family was thrilled as well.

Overall, I was feeling good and chatty and that second night after the surgery, I did not take any painkillers at all.

I was sharing the room with two other patients. They were both ladies. One was very quiet. She was a black lady with a disease that would not allow her to speak or move. She was paralysed from the neck down, and she was under constant care. Her husband would come every evening to visit her and he was praying and playing gospel music on the radio for her.

I remember how her eyes were sometimes gazing at me, almost as if she was trying to say something but could not articulate any words. I wasn't sure if her perceptions were functioning, but I know her soul was there and I could see it in her beautiful eyes. It made me feel so grateful to realise what a blessing is to be aware, and to articulate words and communicate. What a powerful thing that is, and yet we take it for granted.

The other lady was under constant care as well. It made me feel so grateful that I was well and able to eat, speak and move my hands. I was the only patient in that room that was not in such need of care and assistance from others.

At night, trying to sleep was a draining experience. There was always so much noise from the people who were pressing the emergency button for the nurses. It was very hard to get rest there. Sometimes you could hear people who were in pain screaming from other rooms.

But this one night was extra creepy.

It was after midnight when I could hear the nurses whispering about a new emergency coming in. I usually pulled my curtains to keep the light away so that I could get a bit of a rest. After a lot of fuss and noise, a new patient was brought to our room. The screaming was so loud as the nurses tried to accommodate her. It was terrifying just to hear it. She was screaming as if she was in the mouth of a lion. I could not help but feel her pain.

After a while, she went quiet as they managed to keep her calm. Two hours later, she started screaming again as the doctors asked the nurse to take some blood samples from the lady who just had the surgery. This time it was louder and harder than before. I didn't sleep at all that night.

The next day it came to light that this was an 85-year-old lady who had somehow fallen off the balcony. She had multiple injuries to her head and a broken clavicle. It was sad to be surrounded by such cases.

I felt like I didn't belong amongst these people. I felt I was too young to be going through these things, not that anyone at any age should have to go through anything like that anyway. I guess I was scared and just wanted to go home where everything was safe.

The third day after the surgery, the drainage tube that was attached to my head to allow any post-surgery excessive blood out, was finally removed. I felt so relieved and free after that. I knew that any progress in there was another step closer to the day when I'd be going back home.

In the evening, when all the noises faded off and everyone went to sleep, I felt I had a little privacy. I would take this time to thank the universe for this second chance I had been given and for the fact that I was still around. It felt like such a blessing for me to have gone through a successful brain surgery.

During the day, various experts from the neurosurgery team were visiting and checking on my progress. They were pleased to see that I was feeling well and impressed that I was off painkillers so quickly. I am still in awe with the way that my body responded and automatically began the process of healing.

Specialists from the oncology team were also around daily, performing various tests to identify if any of my motor functions, speech and focus had been affected.

I remember them asking me different questions, where I had to focus and use my rational mind to respond correctly. They always used to start by asking me what day it was, the year, and where I was. There were other tasks, like having a few words to focus on and try to remember them, while in the meantime they were asking me other things. At the end I had to recall the words they had mentioned at the beginning. This was a short memory test.

There were also physical tests, aimed at identifying the response and strength of my upper and lower body. For that, I had to push and pull against their arms as they were applying resistance making it harder.

I recall one last expert that visited me at that time, was more of a post-traumatic stress disorder counselling specialist, who gave me her phone number and also asked me if she could call and check on me a few times after I'd be out from the hospital. I guessed she was appointed by the registrar to make sure I was coping well mentally. Much later, after I was back home she did actually call one time now that I remember, and concluded that a second call wasn't needed.

The third day, I got up and walked around the corridors. I remember my sister's face when she saw me standing and slowly walking on my own. She was so surprised. It felt great to be on my feet again. I knew I had a very long way to go, but it felt like I was doing well.

The truth is that I felt strong and was recovering at the speed of light. My own family did not expect to see me talking straight after the surgery. They confessed later that they had thought I'd be sleeping for days. That was not the case at all. I bounced back so quickly. I had a great appetite and that was a sign of vitality. The experts were pleased to see me recovering so quickly and getting back on my feet in such a short time after the surgery.

I was also as "normal" as before, in the sense that I could have a conversation about everything, I could move my body, and there were no motor functions that seemed to have been affected by the surgery. I remembered everything and there were no side effects whatsoever. They finally announced that I could to go home the next day. I was so thrilled!

Later that same day, the nurses removed the head bandage and I could see my whole head for the first time. I was stunned to see how much of my hair had been shaved. However, I was happy that I could see myself in the mirror, alive and smiling. Yes, I could barely recognise myself, but I felt so grateful. My naturally curly hair was so tangled, or what was left of it. Until that moment, I had never thought about how big the wound was. Even though I could not see it properly, it looked huge. It covered a third of my scalp and the line of stitches was covered in orange plasters.

Therefore, I had only two thirds of hair left to untangle. When I looked in the mirror, I could see something between a robot woman and a Star Trek movie character.

I looked so funny. I was laughing at myself, taking selfies with the nurse and sending them over to my family to see the new Marvel character I had become.

BABY STEPS

While I was recovering after surgery in the hospital, my family was planning and adjusting their whole lives and redesigning their homes for me. They were looking for the best ways to better accommodate the remaining part of my healing journey under their care. To be honest, up to that moment, this thought hadn't even crossed my mind. I was blessed that they could take care of all these things for me when I did not have the brains for it.

Formally, I was still liable for the place I was sharing with my flatmate under the lease agreement. Going back to that place was not an option, according to my family. Not at that time, at least. They wanted to keep me under their supervision, so that I could receive the best care and support at home following the discharge from the hospital.

They had agreed that for the first couple of weeks, I would stay at my son's place where it was quieter and calmer compared to where my sister lived, in the middle of London, a few streets from Oxford Street. Later, when I was stronger and the stitches had come off I could move to her place, and take it from there. I was happy with anything, as long as I was out of the hospital. I was so tired of sleeping on that hard bed, having to squat above the toilet seat and washing my body with a wet towel. All I wanted was the comfort of a home, not to mention the peace and quiet, as opposed to the constant noise of a hospital ward.

Finally, after 14 days in a hospital, I was discharged on the 22nd of October 2019, a Friday. My right cheek was still purple and swollen under my eye, but this was considered normal and was something that was going to take some time to heal. Otherwise I was feeling well. I remember waking up early in the morning to get my stuff ready and packed. I had barely slept the night before.

The nurse in charge came to me in the morning and said, "You look very happy to be going home". "Yes, I am!" I replied. "Isn't this the case with every patient leaving the hospital?"

To my surprise she replied, "No, not always. Some patients don't have the care they need at home and no one to look after them. Here, they receive their meals and medication on time. There's always someone to reach out to, if they feel in pain or need anything." That saddened me to hear. It reminded me that some people don't have the things others take for granted.

I recall the feeling I had when I zipped up my small bag and was ready to get out of there. It was pure liberation! It felt like I was walking very slowly but surely towards my freedom. My sisters were waiting for me in the guest room. The nurses came and handed over a bag of medication as prescribed by the neurosurgery team that was monitoring me. The medication consisted of steroids and anti-seizure drugs that would last for a couple of weeks. They briefed my sisters on how to administer the medication and emphasised that we should keep an eye on the wound for any potential infection.

I thanked everyone, and said my goodbyes to all the lovely nurses who had been looking after me. I think I could fill a whole page with the names of all the lovely people that took care of me during that time. I walked out of the hospital with my two sisters' side by side.

It was a beautiful sunny day and the blue sky filled my soul with joy. The fresh air energised my body almost instantly. I was so happy to be out. I felt like a new-born that had just come into the world. It seemed like I had been away from life for so long that I had almost forgotten what it was like to be outdoors. I was very conscious of the fact that I had just had brain surgery and wanted to protect the wound by being very careful of every step I took. I was moving in slow motion all the time. My sisters were very supportive and caring, watching my every move as well, almost as if they knew what I was thinking.

The car was waiting for us at the entrance. I remember that my sister had ordered a luxury taxi ride home. It was very cool, especially when the three of us could easily fit in the back seat. Free treats, drinks and chocolates were included in this ride. How cool is that?!

As we were heading to my son's place, riding in the back of the taxi and watching people, cars, trees, and the city, I remembered how much I'd missed being around people and how much I'd missed my life.

When we arrived, I was so happy to be at home and reunited with my family. My mom also landed that evening. She flew all the way from Romania to be with me and help me heal. We both cried as we were hugging by the doorstep just after she stepped in. I know she was just happy to see me alive. She is the strongest woman I know. I knew she would be alright and that she would do anything to help me get back on my feet.

Being back, I still could not believe what I had just experienced, and felt incredible gratitude for my body and everything that it had been through for me. I felt fortunate to be strong enough to walk on my own, hug my loved ones, and communicate with them.

I was well but still needed help with everything, such as bathing myself and dressing up. Obviously, I had to be very cautious not to hurt my head by mistake or push against the stitched wound, as it was still very fresh after the surgery. I had to wear large tops so I didn't have to squeeze my head through.

The first thing I did after returning home that day, was to take a shower in the comfort of a clean home bathroom after so long. That was relaxing and comforting. I felt like a whole new person after that. And yes, sometimes the little pleasures of life include sitting on your own toilet without having to worry about keeping your balance while squatting above the toilet seat with a bandaged head.

While I was in the hospital, the one thing I had felt most deprived of, was a good sleep. From the day I had been admitted until 14 days later, I had not had one single night of proper rest. There was always someone screaming, buzzing, talking or checking my vitals. Lack of sleep always makes me feel weaker, and rest is a key factor in one's healing process.

That first night, I think I had the best sleep of my entire life. My family had researched and purchased the best pillows, bed covers and everything that would ensure my comfort and could support the only position I was able to rest my head at the time. I literally had a "nest" that resembled a puffy cloud.

Back then, I could only sleep in a reclined position where I would feel comfortable enough to fall asleep and get some rest. I could not lay flat or on my right side at all, or even twist a bit. It's hard to recover when you are forced to sleep in a particular position, which is normal after such major surgery. However, the fact that I was home, and undisturbed, made a huge difference. When I woke up, I felt incredibly refreshed and revitalised, which was something I hadn't felt in a very long time.

It was so nourishing for my body to enjoy the delicious home-made food my family had put together for me every day. I could eat on my own, even though, for the first few days, there was a numbness on the left side of my mouth and sometimes I could not feel my lip on that side. For that reason, I didn't use any cutlery to avoid hurting myself, so I was using my fingers to eat for a few days, until the numbness disappeared.

My family was my rock. They were always on top of my medication, the timings and the combinations in which I had to take everything. They cooked, looked after me, and made sure that I had a meal every time. I did not have to worry about any of it.

The place was so clean, you could have had an operation in there. I recollect hearing my son hoovering and mopping the floor every night after I went to bed to make sure everything was in perfect clean condition.

During the first few days back at home, I was just eating and napping. It was so weird. I would be awake for half an hour then I would just drift into a very deep sleep for twenty minutes each time. After that, I'd be back up, continuing the same pattern. This was a pattern that would repeat itself throughout the day. My brain needed all the rest and rebooting it could get.

For example, I would be lying on the couch listening to my mum and my sisters chatting, and I would follow and even join in with the conversation as well, but after a while, I would suddenly feel the need to shut my eyes as my focus was completely gone, and I could not keep up. It was literally a forced switch off that my brain needed, and I was instantly drifting away. It was totally out of my control.

After a few good night's sleeps, I was feeling much better. I felt more alert and focused. I was even strong enough to make my way into the kitchen and help my middle sister cook dinner. Basically, I was just stirring the food in the pan but it felt good to be able to do that, and she was happy to see me up and doing that as well. I was still on a small quantity of steroids, but they were working, so my appetite was still very good.

One night around 2 am, I woke up feeling very hungry. I got out of my bed and very slowly made my way to the kitchen looking for something to eat. My son heard me and he jumped up worried that something happened. I remember whispering to him, "I was just looking for some food". I remembered I had some of the fresh olive bread roll that they had bought for me that day, so I ate it and went to bed again.

Of course, my son wanted to make sure that this didn't happen again, as he was worried I might hurt myself. Therefore, the following evening, he made sure I had plenty of snacks by my bedside, in case I got hungry again and went wandering around the kitchen in the middle of the night.

I marvel every time I think about how the human body can bounce back so quickly after such shocking and traumatic events. Even though we feel fragile and we try to protect ourselves, the human body is much stronger and more resilient than we can ever imagine.

I remember when I sneezed for the first time after the surgery. I felt it coming but could not hold it in anymore. It wasn't major, in fact a tiny one, but it happened and certainly felt the stitches in my head with that sneeze. Something similar happened when I swallowed a minor fragment of food down the airway and had to cough a few times; it was painful. The struggle was real, as they say.

There was also another thing that I could not do, or rather, did not feel the need to do, until, after a while: the automatic stretching of your body as you wake up in the morning. It took a while before I felt the need to do that and, when I did, it felt like I was a little baby stretching my body for the first time in my life.

Yawning was a weird one as well. I could not open my mouth fully. My jaw was still too tight. I remember the experts telling me how important it was to move my jaw and masticate the food carefully just to get movement at that joint, and to encourage blood flow. I had been experiencing a bit of stiffness around the right side of my jaw after the surgery while I was still in the hospital but it got better after about a week. It was no wonder, since my jaw had been wide open during the long hours of the entire surgery, as they had to place the oxygen tubes down my throat.

The funny thing was that I did not feel the need to yawn until weeks after the surgery. It was almost as if my body knew I should not do that.

These are the little things that we normally don't even think about. We cough, we sneeze, we stretch as part of our normal daily functioning but it's all connected to our nervous system. To me it's just magical when I think of how it all works for us without any conscious decision on our part. In my case, it kept me from doing some things, until it was safe enough. The body just knows.

I was advised to move daily, as part of the recovery process. The first week wasn't a great one in terms of weather. But when the sun came out, we decided to go out for a walk.

We were by the river and the sun was shining in such a special way that day. When I went out just walking and holding my son's arm, I got all emotional. It felt so humbling and beautiful. I was just standing there looking at the sun and the reflection of its light in the river. It was magical. I realised how much I had missed my freedom. I remembered how close I am to nature and how much I need it in my life.

Physically I was seeing progress every day. It felt like my body was stronger and more confident. Friends also started to come by. I was so happy to see my close friends and godson from Cyprus who heard the sudden news. They came to visit me as soon as they had a chance. These people are friends that I am blessed to call family and I was so happy to hug them again. I knew that for them, as for all my friends that came to see me around those days, I was always a picture of health, someone they'd look up to and get inspiration from. At least to that point.

A part of me did not want them to see me like that. I thought that it must be as hard for them as it was for me. We'd talk about old times and how they were happy to see me standing there after this crazy turn of events. I'd still get tired very quickly after a short interaction with them. Half an hour was all I could manage. After that I had to reboot again.

On the other side of the coin, recovering mentally and emotionally after such a traumatic experience seemed like a slow process and a difficult place to be at the time. It is confusing to lose your identity, or better said, that which you think is your identity.

As I was walking by the mirrors in the house, it was getting harder for me to look at myself, as I could not recognise my own reflection. It wasn't at all the image I was used to. To be honest, from the first day of the surgery until that day, my face was different every single time I looked into the mirror. It was changing constantly.

I had similar features but they were distorted in my view. It was another challenging phase. I also knew it was hard for my loved ones to see me in that situation, and by that I don't just mean the external appearance. But also seeing a loved one going through a brain surgery with stitches, bandages and a swollen head, being fragile and vulnerable. They were my family and I know they were all just happy to have me there, alive, considering all that could have happened.

I guess… I was the one who was really having a hard time seeing myself in that situation and therefore not wanting anyone else to experience that feeling. It made me realise that I wasn't used to show my vulnerability to others and to receive so much help. But now, I had to learn to give myself permission and to allow myself to be vulnerable and to receive all the help I could get. What a lesson!

The good part was that my body was getting better day by day. I particularly remember one Sunday afternoon. We had our family lunch and hung about together. I wasn't sleeping as often during the day by that time. I felt so well that I remember telling my little sister, If I had a treadmill right now, I'd probably get on it. She smiled and said it was probably from all the steroids I was still taking.

Before I knew it, the day came to remove the stitches. I was so excited to have that done, and it all went fine. I had no pain whatsoever. The nurse also happened to be a friend, to whom I had been introduced to by another very close friend of mine, just after I was admitted to Kings. The moment she heard what had happened, she had called her friend, a head nurse who was working in the oncology department, and asked her to be my guardian angel while I was there. And she was!

At the appointment, she was very pleased to see me recovering so quickly the way that I did. When she took the bandage off she was happily surprised to see that it was perfectly clean and the wound was healing beautifully. She was very gentle, I could barely feel anything. I remember my sister holding my hand, as the nurse was removing all 42 or so stitches one by one.

That day was the first time when I was able to closely look at the actual size of the wound from a different angle. My sister took a picture with her phone. She said, "Are you ready to see this; are you sure you want to see it?" Yes, I was, but when I did, I was shocked by the size of it. Imagine 42 stitches. It was almost all the right side of my head to the level of my ear. It was so unbelievable to actually see that such a big part of my head had literally been cracked.

I was pleased however to have ticked off that step of the process. My head seemed to have felt much lighter and free that day after taking the stitches out. I thought to myself, I am on the straight road to recovery. I was looking forward to washing my hair too.

That same afternoon, when we got back home, I received a call from the neurology team that was looking after my case. I was supposed to have an appointment but they had good news and they called instead. I was extremely happy to hear that the biopsy confirmed that the growth they removed was non-malignant and that it was unlikely to return. Such great news. They did mention however, that they would keep an eye on me, by monitoring yearly as the protocol suggests.

They told me to stay off exercise for six weeks after which I could reintroduce everything slowly. I was pleased to hear the good news. She gave me her contact number in case I needed her for any reason during that time.

The day after, I moved to my sister's place. She had my room ready and everything to keep me safe and comfortable. My mom was cooking and looking after me as usual. My middle sister had gone back to Sweden so my mum and little sister were fully in charge of the situation.

I remember two days after I took the stitches off, we decided to go for some fresh air. It was a beautiful day. I loved the rose garden in Regent's Park, so I took my mom there as I knew she would enjoy that. I remember wrapping my head well and wearing a winter coat and the hoodie under that. I was off any medication by that time and was feeling well. I was able to walk without much assistance. It was a blessing to enjoy that time with my mother and to be out in nature again. We sat on a bench and I laid the left side of my head on her lap trying to rest a bit before heading it back home again.

That evening I finally washed my hair after almost a month. The nurse said that I could do that now that the stitches were off. I had almost forgotten how nice and fresh that felt.

A couple of days later, my face started to look a bit more swollen than it usually did. My right eye seemed more bruised again. I thought the swelling was normal after brain surgery and that is what I was told. I mentioned it to the doctors, but it was nothing out of the ordinary and it all seemed to be normal after such an operation.

My appetite was still very good and my mom was spoiling me in all ways possible. We even cooked together one day. We made Greek pastitsio and pecan pie, my recipes, but my mom was mostly executing them. I was just guiding her.

That day I remember, I had a tight neck; it was slightly stiff but I could still move it. That was just a few days after I had the stitches removed. I thought it was from the way I had slept which was still in the same position since the surgery. But it turned out that wasn't the case. A stiff neck is one of the signs that I missed. It is a sign of infection. However, by the time you feel that, it's already kind of late.

THE HURRICANE

Sometimes our experiences are just a result of some uncontrollable series of events that happen within this universe with such speed, precision and intensity, that it is impossible for us to even begin to stop them. I was living my worst nightmare; the following day, on the 5th of November, Tuesday evening around 6 pm, when I was talking to my nephew, who had just got back from school, and he said, "Mari, there is something oozing from the wound near your ear".

I instantly reached to touch my ear, and I felt a wet texture on my fingertips. That moment, I thought my heart had stopped. I felt dizzy straight away from the intense panic. I grabbed a tissue to wipe that off and then another one, which I kept pressed against the wound, until I could come to my senses and work out what to do next. The fluid was a light orange colour and it was abundant enough to get me change the tissues quite often. I told my mum that something was wrong and I could see her panicking as well.

I didn't know what to do. I was just walking up and down the room. I'm still not sure how it came to me in that shocking state, but somehow, I "received" a moment of clarity and remembered that I'd written down the number of the support team.

My hands were shaking as I pressed the numbers on the screen of my phone to make the call. My heart was begging the whole universe, "please pick up, please pick up," every time the phone rang. I am so glad that I called, right at that moment, because when she picked up she told me that they were just about to go home for the day. With my voice trembling, I explained what had just happened.

She asked me if I could send a picture of the wound to her email. I asked my nephew who was just next to me, to help me do that. This was happening so fast. The image got through straight away and they confirmed that it looked like an infection. My heart was racing like never before. She suggested that I find a way to go to the A&E immediately and ask for a particular doctor. I wrote his name on a piece of paper. I folded that and put it in my pocket.

Before we hung up, she said, "Do not eat any food, just drink water". My heart stopped again. I knew what that meant. Potentially another surgery. I was literally shaking and felt like a zombie walking. I could not believe what was happening. It was the most traumatising experience I'd ever had in my entire life.

We dropped everything and jumped into a taxi to the hospital. My heart was still racing like crazy. I felt so disheartened and disappointed, but all I was trying to do is make my mum feel better and act like it wasn't as bad as it seemed. That was not how I really felt. Every now and then, I'd check my pocket to see if the paper with the name of the doctor was still in there.

When we arrived, there were so many people waiting to be seen. I pulled the note out of my pocket and showed it to the receptionist as I went through the registration. While I was waiting, I called my son and my sister, to let them know what had just happened. Everyone was still at work, but as soon as they finished, they came as well.

Finally, after a long wait, the doctors showed up. They examined me and confirmed that there was an infection. The nurse was taking samples of the pus, for the lab. It was still dripping. In the distance, I could see my mum crying as she was talking to my son.

The doctor who came to examine me, was Greek and we exchanged a few words in his native language. My family gathered around the examination bed where I was lying as he was explaining in detail what was happening.

They wanted to admit me immediately and have a scan to see the extent of the infection. He explained all the scenarios. If the infection was superficial they would just give me antibiotics, but if it was more serious, they would have to "open" me again, and wash the wound. Basically, another operation. I could not believe what I was hearing. It was my worst nightmare coming true. I felt devastated. My mother could not understand English, so my son translated what the doctor had said into Romanian for her. I could see and feel her anxiety as she was listening to him.

The nurse in charge at the emergency shift, made a request for any available bed in the other wards of the hospital. They asked me to wait until they would confirm their availability for me to be admitted. My family was still around after waiting for hours, and by that time, it must have been past 10 pm. I kept telling them to go home but of course they wouldn't. I wasn't in any physical pain and I was conscious and aware of everything, but I was completely shattered inside.

In the meantime, the nurse was taking blood samples and re-dressing the wound which was still discharging fluids. Half an hour later, one of the wards confirmed that they had one available bed and that they were happy to take me in. In all my despair, the universe had at least given me something to hold on. The bed they had for me was exactly the one I had left three weeks earlier, on the same floor, same room. Bed 17.

I left my family and told them not to worry about me, and that I would be OK and keep them updated. But in reality, I was terrified. This time I was really worried that something might go wrong.

The nurse guided me upstairs and there I was, walking again into that ward. I felt completely devastated, but a part of me felt some mild comfort when I saw their familiar faces. I knew all of them. Their warm welcome and genuine sympathy added a drop of honey to my bitter glass.

As much as I didn't want to be there, I felt safe in that environment, as I knew I was in good hands. In fact, just the day before this happened, I'd sent an email to the head of the ward, a lovely lady, just to express my gratitude to all the people that had looked after me while I was recovering after the surgery. I truly could not believe the fact that I had just returned to that place again. What a nightmare.

As I was getting settled, I noticed the dark that was surrounding me, the fragile people lying there and my soul drifted into sadness. I didn't lie down, but sat on the side of the bed, pressing the patch against my leaking wound and waiting to hear from the experts. I was told they would come to see me any moment. And it did not take long. This time, the lead neurosurgeon was there, which was a rare occasion. He personally came to my bed and explained all the steps.

He said that I was due to have an operation so they could wash the wound. That was established. He continued to explain that since they would be opening the skull again they would have to flip the flap bone and check if the infection had affected the other side, as there was a big chance of that being the case.

If that was the situation, then they would leave it out as it would endanger my condition. "What do you mean", I asked? "I will lose it, and have no skull around that area?" And he replied, "Yes, for a while, there would be no flap bone, until we arrange another surgery to close the wound with a metal plate." In that instant, I felt like the whole building was starting to crash on me from all directions. I could not believe what I was hearing.

I felt like a sudden furious storm had just started to blow again and I was soaking in a cold heavy rain. I did not know where to find shelter, nor did I have the strength to resist it in any way. I was on my knees in the middle of the hurricane holding my head with trembling hands and my heart torn apart.

Later that night as all went quiet, I was thinking about everything that the doctors told me. I was terrified of the whole idea of having another surgery, but not only that. It was also the thought that there could be a third surgery sometime in the future. I was feeling like I was standing at the bottom of the tallest mountain looking at the peak and had no idea how I was ever going to get at the top. It seemed impossible.

I felt completely devastated, I wanted to scream at the universe; What lesson am I supposed to learn from this? You saved me once and now this again, so soon after. What did I do wrong? Am I being punished for something? I don't understand. Wasn't that enough already?

More arguments and questions were spinning in my mind as I was waiting for the nurse to pick me up for the MRI scan. How was it possible that I had shown no obvious signs of infection like fever or other serious symptoms?

How was it possible to get an infection; what were the odds of this? My home was so clean, you could perform a surgery in there. The wound had been looking fine, healing beautifully. The doctors that saw it had confirmed it. I had been extra cautious with everything. I had only been wearing the best quality clothes, head scarves made of 100% Egyptian cotton, and avoiding any washing products that contained chemicals. I had been eating well and using only organic products.

Once again, I started to blame to myself: "I should have read more about the signs. If I had gone to see the doctors a couple of days ago when my neck was stiff maybe I could have avoided this. But how is it possible for this infection to have happened, just in the past few days after I had the stitches out. There was no way that this had happened in just a few days."

When your head is opened for six hours and your bone flap sits outside of your body and then it's put back and your skin stitched on top of that, I guess there is a big chance for an infection to happen. It is in fact one of the risks I had signed off, way before the surgery and they had kept mentioning to keep an eye on it, when I went home.

The lowest point of these cascade of emotions, was when I began to worry with thoughts like, "What if something happens to me? What if something suddenly goes wrong? What if I am going to die?"

I especially recall that moment, because there was an avalanche of feelings that crashed down on me. I wasn't only scared because my life could end, but also because people I love would have to suffer because of it.

A tremendous wave of mixed feelings of sorrow and gratitude came over me. I remembered the deep connection I shared with my family and all my wonderful friends. How fortunate I was to have so much love in my life. I felt my heart breaking with the thought that it might all come to an end. If that was going to be it for me, and I was to be gone, my whole existence was just screaming; "But I need more time! Please, I need at least one more chance to tell them how much I love them."

My heart was sizzling with fire, and a river of burning tears started sliding down my face. There was so much more I wanted to do with them. There was so much more I wanted to tell them. So many places I wanted to visit with them, like my dream of a full family holiday to a wonderful place like Hawaii.

Then I remembered; "Oh, my heart, my son's wedding!" The day was set for May 2021 in Bali. I remember the heavy tears almost choking me as I thought, "I can't miss it; I have to walk him down the aisle on that day. I have to be there. I can't leave him alone. Not now, not yet. Please, I have to make it, I have to."

My whole existence was spinning in a hurricane of pain and fear. It was taking everything with it and I could not find any shelter. Between the relentless blast of the furious wind and heavy rainstorm, I could see the willow tree in the distance. I struggled to run and get there and when I finally did, I clenched my arms tightly around its trunk. I didn't know if I had enough strength to hold on and save myself from the fury of that hurricane.

My eyes were tightly shut as I held on with all my strength. The thuds of the powerful storm were terrifying. It sounded like everything was snapping and disintegrating in the face of it. My heart was shrinking with fear. Through my tears and prayers, I could vaguely hear the whispers of the willow tree, while its branches were completely surrendering to the furious wind, *"Don't be afraid to surrender, look… its OK, have faith, it will be all right, you'll see."* It took a while before the hurricane slowly started to move further and further away and the noise began to fade. The gravity finally took over the branches of the willow tree and as they naturally fell towards the ground, they gently touched my face as I opened my eyes. We were safe.

It is in these moments when you truly understand, that one lifetime is not enough to spend with the people you love and to show them how much they mean to you. You understand that when the last moment is close, it all comes down to one single thing. How much love you allowed yourself to experience in your life. Nothing else matters. All the success and the material things you have acquired in your life, won't mean a thing. All that matters, is that your heart feels full with love.

The peak of this wave of emotions came after all those tears. It was when I seem to have received the answer to many questions that were still swirling around my mind.

"How was it possible that even though the skin was healed and sealed in every spot all around the cut, it had still found a tiny dot to make its way out. What if that little opened 'dot' hadn't been there? Where would all the discharge have gone? What would have happened then?"

In that instant, all my questions about being given a lesson or being punished suddenly vanished. I could clearly see the answer. If the wound had not begun to release the pus, there would have been no way to know that I had an infection, because I had no obvious symptoms. I would probably have found out much later, when the infection could have spread everywhere and caused serious damage to my whole system.

The thought of it blew my mind! It would have been fatal. That realisation made me feel incredibly humble. A divine blanket of warm love covered my broken heart, which was still trembling with fear.

Something started to shift within, and I began to see the blessing even more clearly. Whatever the reason for what was happening, I somehow began to feel convinced that I was given a double second chance.

A chance to let go of any expectations or need to control, and to surrender to something that is greater than myself. A chance to upgrade my faith levels, and to allow the universe to propel me forward.

The certain thing is, that we can't control everything in life. Some things happen unexpectedly and you have to adjust your sails. If you try to resist the strong currents, you'll break.

You learn to become like a willow tree, flexible and resilient. No matter how strong the wind blows, the willow tree won't break because it becomes part of the storm by dancing with the wind.

That means you have to find a way to accept and honour what is in front of you, without any hope or wish to control what happens in the end.

Just make your way through and do your best. There is great strength when you can surrender to what is, accept it exactly the way it is, and learn to ride the wave moment by moment.

I remembered that when I had first found out about the diagnosis, had the surgery and as I had been trying to figure out my way forward, I had decided to take everything step by step. The catch was, that I had never expected that the next step was another surgery. I had been hoping for a smoother journey. But again, we can't see what's coming ahead, we can only deal with what is in front of us.

As I was still overwhelmed by the revelation of the blessing in disguise and I was allowing all the dust to settle, the nurse came in and told me it was time for the MRI scan. I could walk so I didn't need a wheelchair. I remember having to stay still for 30 minutes in that tube while trying to keep sane. It was so noisy and I was physically and emotionally exhausted. It made me remember all the struggles of the surgery that were just waiting for me around the corner.

She took me back to the room. I felt shattered by the nightmare I was living, but at the same time, I felt safe.

THE LIGHT IN THE DARKNESS

I remember laying in that bed, looking up at the ceiling while the red light was bleeping on the hospital corridors. Even though somehow numb, a part of me was silently repeating; *"I am so grateful, I am so blessed, I am so grateful, I am so blessed"*. As I was mumbling these words, my face and neck were drowning in tears. The more I repeated it, the heavier the tears would get. That moment, felt as if a river had arrived to the point where it meets the sea, and it began to fall into a cascade. Emotions of fear and pain, slowly turned into gratitude, hope and faith.

My heart began to sing a silent melody hoping that someone up there can hear it:

"Thank you for not giving up on me when I was kneeling in the mud. Thank you for shining your light on me. When everything was pitch dark and I almost lost hope, I saw your mighty light flickering slowly in the dark. As it was flickering, my soul began to flicker with it too, and then I felt your love. My heart began to fill with hope and then hope turned into belief and belief into faith. *And there it was, Your Mighty Light in my greatest darkness.*

Now I could see that even though on the outside I may have resembled something of a broken doll, that didn't matter at all. What mattered, was that I felt whole and bright on the inside.

I now know what true beauty is and what unwavering faith means. Why did I ever think that I was less than that, when Your law is carved into my own existence? How could I have not seen that before? How could I have been so blind? You were always there with me. Thank you. Thank you. Thank you. You came to save me. A lost sheep in the darkness."

I felt connected with God many times before, but that was one of the deepest spiritual experiences I had to that point in my life. Even in the hardest times, you can still find something to be grateful for. The source of life that shines within you is there to give you something to hold on to when you most need it. That is when you learn to surrender and allow the universe to take over what lies ahead.

That moment, I realised that whatever this experience was about, and no matter how bad it seemed to be, I knew that I would come out of it.

I understood that, at the core, we are all built to endure anything that life brings us. And it's never about what seemingly happens on the outside; that is always misleading. It's always about how we feel inside and how much our heart is willing to move on. I had taken a very long journey to come to this conclusion.

When my face dried and my soul felt lighter, I began to notice what was happening around me in the ward. I noticed that the two old ladies, the one that was paralysed and the 85-year- old, were still there in the same beds. It felt sad to see that. Again, I felt like I didn't belong there. I was tired, hungry and dehydrated as I drifted into sleep.

Around 3 am in the morning, a soft voice woke me up. It was the lead surgeon that had performed my first surgery, Anna. I had never met her before, but I knew her name. She came by to tell me that I was soon going to be taken to the theatre. She also expressed how sorry she was that I caught the infection. She had been extremely happy with the initial operation. She told me how pleased she had been when she managed to completely remove the whole thing and then stitched everything so nicely and it all looked so promising. "Yes, who would have thought!" I said to her.

Whispering, I asked if she would be performing this surgery on me. She nodded her head. I was so pleased to hear that and it gave me a soft sense of reassurance. I trusted her, as I knew she had saved my life before. We went through the usual paperwork, I signed it off and then she left me saying that she'd send for me soon. I fell back asleep, exhausted from everything.

Around 6 am, the nurse woke me up, softly saying that the surgeon was ready for me. An assistant and another nurse began to roll my bed along the corridors to the theatre. This time the operation room was spacious and they could easily get my bed through the doors. They asked me a few questions, and before you know it I was out for the second time in less than one month. If you had told me this story before I lived through it, I'd have told you it was a very bad joke.

A NEW HOPE

When I opened my eyes, I was in the recovery room again. This time I wasn't feeling confused. I knew straight away where I was. The nurse was lovely and was talking me through what had happened, which was very similar with the first time. I was feeling weak and my head was hurting. She confirmed that I had no bone flap, which meant I was definitely due for another surgery in the near future. I felt disheartened when she confirmed that. But on the bright side, at least I was still alive and aware of my environment.

I was taken back to the ward and immediately placed under very intensive care and close supervision. Due to the severity of the infection, I was prescribed strong intravenous antibiotics every eight hours. That required needles and tubes going into my veins to administer the chemicals straight into my blood stream. There were two types of antibiotics. One of them was Vancomycin, which is one of the strongest available for serious infections. It can have damaging side effects on your kidneys and ears.

The other one was milder and in a smaller dosage; they would mix the antibiotic in a large saline water bag. They would hang that fluid bag to a standing support and then would attach the wires to an electronic gadget also placed on that support, which controlled the speed at which the fluid flowed through the tubes into my veins.

I recall that one of the infusion bags was hanging there for almost three hours. The other one would last about 30 minutes. These chemicals were so strong, to the point that it felt like my veins were on fire at times. They were taking my blood every 12 hours to monitor how the bacteria reacted to the antibiotics and to see how my vitals were functioning with so much going on in my body. This was also a precautionary step to ensure that my liver and kidneys were not being affected by the strong antibiotics. If the tests were abnormal, they would then adjust the dose. Luckily, that never happened, so I thank my kidneys and liver for dealing with all the chaos without creating any more issues.

The first few days after the surgery, I felt incredibly weak, like never before. I couldn't get out of bed for days. I was sleeping most of the time. My appetite wasn't as great as it had been the previous time. I did not have the strength to go to the toilet on my own and I needed assistance with that. They literally brought "the toilet" to me if you know what I mean, as I wasn't strong enough to walk to it myself.

The right side of my head was swollen out of proportion. That was mainly because there was no bone flap and so much fluid was accumulated around the brain. It was something that the body naturally does and it was going to take quite a while before the inflammation would retract. At least that was what the experts were saying.

In other words, I had half an elephant head. I was feeling vulnerable and exposed because of the missing flap of bone. My stamina was incredibly low, I couldn't even stand on my feet for more 20 seconds, or stay awake for longer that 15 minutes. It was a very low point in my whole journey to recovery. To be completely transparent, up to that point in my life, I had never felt that powerless.

The experts visited every day, updated me on the results of the tests and checked the wound. My vitals looked good and despite the obvious, things were looking hopeful.

After a few days, when I could manage to get out of bed, I remember waking up in the morning, taking a few steps across the corridor to the toilet where I would freshen up and brush my teeth. By the time I'd done that and got back to the room, I'd already feel tired and my heart rate would shoot up. The moment I'd speak or move my arms even for a bit, it would get even faster. To be precise, it was somewhere between 95 and

121 heartbeats per minute, when I was laying down. I know this because I was strapped with a heart monitor almost all the time.

My body was feeling it in every sense. I was thinking what turmoil it must be for my body, going through another surgery and all the chemicals. Whenever I had that thought, I was giving my thanks and gratitude to that divine force that had to be at play for me to still be around.

My family was visiting regularly; I remember how I'd slowly open my eyes after those consistent doses of sleep, and I'd get to see the beautiful faces and loving smiles of my son and his fiancée, who were patiently seated by my bed and watching over me while I was sleeping. That always made my heart smile in an instant. Luckily, my mum was also there for me to keep me going. She would cook for me and carry the food to the hospital every single day. She was living for that. She would make sure to arrive just in time for lunch. If it happened that I was asleep, she'd wait until I woke up and then she would "feed me". It is incredible how being surrounded by the love of family can actually speed the healing process. I have read this somewhere that a whole study was done around this subject. It is a fact that when little babies are sick, they heal quicker when the mother holds them in their arms and the symptoms, such as fever for example, disappear.

I don't remember spending so much time in bed before in my whole life. I was trying to take a few steps every day, but it wasn't easy at the beginning. As a result, my body felt stiff and was hurting everywhere from lack of movement. I recall my mum and my little sister came one evening to bring me dinner and they also brought some oil to massage my feet and legs.

They could see that everything was harder for me this time around and they were doing their best to comfort me while I was there. Watching them gently massaging my feet, mum on the left and my sister on the right side, and feeling the energy of love and care almost brought tears to my eyes; it felt so nice for my aching body. It seemed impossible to get proper rest and sleep in the hospital, especially when you are injected and monitored constantly. I wasn't getting much rest overall, but that night, after the gentle massage, I slept much better.

As I was slowly improving, some friends started to visit me as well. I was happy to see my flatmate, who came to visit one day. I was missing her and my place as well. My family was considering whether, after I was to be discharged, I could move back to my place with my flatmate and my mum could stay there with me as well, for as long as needed. The place was big enough for the three of us, and we would each still have our own room. They knew that I'd love it by the river and that it would be better for my healing process. I was very happy with that and could not wait for that day to come.

When I sensed I had a bit more energy, I knew things were getting better because my appetite was slowly coming back as well. It wasn't as strong as the first time, but it was still a good sign.

Luckily, I have a close friend who was regularly coming to visit me and she'd always made sure to spoil me with whatever I was craving. I remember when she could see that the "excitement" was getting me a bit tired, she would just hold my hand saying: "Don't worry my lovely, just close your eyes and rest for a minute, I will be here by your side." I felt blessed.

My family was bringing me bottled water, fruits and good quality home-made foods every day. Eating well and hydrating definitely helped my body a great deal. It was incredible to see how it slowly builds itself back up and how much energy from food the immune system needs to do that.

During this critical time for my health, I knew the damaging side effects of the chemicals that were entering my body on a daily basis. Therefore, I was consciously looking for ways to help myself. I remember drinking warm water mixed with lemon juice and honey in the morning. Other times I would have cinnamon tea, which was made by infusing a cinnamon stick in hot water. This was with the intention to naturally detox and help my body release all the chemical residues, so that all my organs could function better and I could thus assist the healing process. Needless to say, I was very fortunate that my family could provide everything I needed to be able to do that while still in the hospital.

Since I was careful with my diet, I also decided to exclude any dairy products, as I knew that it can cause even more inflammation in the body, and I had enough of that going on at the time. Drinking much water really helped, especially my kidneys and liver with the amount of antibiotics and chemicals I was taking. It was flushing all the toxicity and residuals out, revitalising and refreshing every cell in my body.

My emotional and mental health were very fragile. It was taxing me at every level. I wasn't crying as much as I had before the surgery, but I felt low. I was seeking ways to soothe my soul and find that inner peace. Prayer, music and meditation always helped me. Every night before I went to sleep and after waking up in the morning, I would listen to my favourite calming music and healing meditation frequencies. I would also silently repeat powerful healing affirmations. I didn't just mumble the words, but I felt these words in my body. I knew how important all these practices are to the process of healing and I always felt a mental boost afterward.

About a week after the surgery, my stamina was slowly increasing and I was feeling better physically. I could move more and the experts were giving me promising news on my progress.

THE STRUGGLE

The thing that got to me the most wasn't the pain of the surgical wound, if you can believe it. I had barely taken any painkillers ever since the first operation and the headaches had been completely gone.

The real struggle was the pain from all the needles my arms were taking every time I had to have my blood sample taken and antibiotics administered. After a week of having intravenous fluids three times a day for several hours, it got unbearable. Every bit of my arms was bruised and aching. I remember touching my forearm with my fingertips; it did not feel soft like skin and flesh anymore. It felt like a piece of wood, hard and ridged; it was so painful just to touch. Not to mention that it was all bruised and pierced by needles. It was the kind of pain that makes you want to cry.

The toxicity, coupled with the frequent use of these chemicals, was making my veins and tissues congest. This type of medication is ideally dispensed through an internal catheter called a PICC line, standing for peripheral inserted central catheter, ideal for extended use. It is a very thin, long tube inserted into a central large vein near the heart. This would have avoided the pain of frequent needles and irritation of the smaller veins, which was happening in my case.

The doctors knew that I needed this gadget for the type of medication that I was being given, and I was booked and due to have this procedure very soon, but I was told that there were many people waiting for this before me. In the meantime, they had to administer all the medication through a regular cannula.

A cannula is a medical gadget, widely used to draw blood or insert a transfusion directly into the bloodstream. There is no tube on the inside of your body, just a short plastic needle that stays inside a smaller vein, with the thin tube hanging on the outside. At the end of this short tube, there is a plastic filament. The dosage of antibiotic or any fluid that needs to be administered is attached to that filament. It can sometimes be an injection or a fluid bag.

I was patiently waiting for my turn, but it all became too painful. The nurse was supposed to administer the antibiotics through the cannula that had already been used for the previous dose, but, by the moment the antibiotic would flow through the tubes into my veins, the pain was intolerable. My flesh was just screaming. I wanted to cry like a baby. Usually, if I could take it for a minute, then it would stop. It had worked before, but this time was impossible, my veins were sealed. That was the last dose I needed to take using this gadget before my appointment to insert the PICC line, but it was too painful. I called the nurse and asked her to remove it immediately. I was literally crying from the pain. Imagine that, I had almost 50 stitches in my head, and I was crying over something else. She was very kind and understanding, and she carefully removed it for me. We tried to find another spot to add a new one so that I could take this last dose, but there were no more intact veins left. That's how messed up my arms were by that point. My entire body felt so invaded.

They made a few calls and managed to get me a spot for that procedure a few hours before my time. I was extremely happy to hear this, as I had been getting worried about being behind with the treatment. They assured me that the process took less than 30 minutes and that it wouldn't be a problem for my dose of the antibiotics.

A chaperone came with a wheelchair to take me to the ground floor where I would have this PICC line procedure. I loved the brightness of that room. As I laid on the bed, I could see outside the window. It was so calming and relaxing when I could also hear some music playing in the background. They gave me a local anaesthesia on my bicep, to avoid feeling any pain from the procedure. That's where it was implanted. I could not believe it when they literally inserted a 44 cm thin plastic tube through the central vein in my arm and pushed that through until it was close enough to my heart. They were doing this using specialised equipment and I could see this through a monitor. It was the first time I had anything like this done. It was mind blowing to me. I could not feel a thing and, even better, it was a very short process so I could have my dose of antibiotics straight after without further delay.

It was such a relief not to be in agony anymore. There was no need to be pierced again, as they could now just draw blood and administer the antibiotics through that device every time. That was such a game changer. I felt like something heavy had lifted off my chest. I slept better, without the fear of the excruciating pain that night.

Every morning, someone from the neurosurgery team would come to check on me and update me on my progress based on the ongoing tests. The plan was to continue with these strong antibiotics for about ten days in total, by when they expected that the infection would retract. If that was successful, they would switch me to a milder dose of intravenous medication for the remainder of the four weeks. That was just to make sure that everything was properly healed before I was off medication completely.

One morning something strange but great at the same time happened. I woke up and could still remember a scary dream I had just had. As you already know by now, I'm into deciphering them. I dreamed of a huge black snake, like an anaconda. It was abnormally big and frightening. However, in my dream, this snake just slid away and disappeared. As I woke up, I said to myself, "I hope the snake is not a bad omen, even though it looked very scary and black… but I think the fact that it did not harm me and went away, should be a good sign."

Incredibly, less than an hour later, it turned out it was a good omen indeed. Around 9 am when the doctors did their rounds on the ward and came by to see me, I received great news. According to the blood tests, the infection had started to recede and things were looking good. They informed me that they had arranged for me to have a head scan, to see how much the infection had reduced and to plan the next steps forward. I was so thrilled to hear that. I called my family and told them the good news straight away. Finally, things were starting to look better.

Every night before going to sleep, besides listening to calming music and repeating positive affirmations, I was also silently praying and talking to my spirit guides giving them my thanks for all the good things in my life. As a little girl, I had been taught that there was a little angel watching over me and I should thank him every night. I confess that growing up, I may have not always remembered to action that. However, I have always believed that I had my own angel watching over me. Often enough throughout my life, I found myself giving thanks to God for sending me his guardian angels. For the past few years, I had been particularly drawn to one of them, Archangel Raphael. He is known as one of the seven holy angels and revered for his healing energies. In fact, I had this beautiful emerald-like angel image as a screen saver on my phone. This was way before this crisis. I always felt connected with that energy somehow.

Looking back from the first day when I laid my head on that hospital bed, through the first surgery and then the second, I realised how incredibly magic this whole journey was. I had literally got up on my feet from something the doctors couldn't guarantee that I would. I was convinced that I had immense grace from all the healing love that I received through the prayers of my family and loved ones and all the divine energies around me.

Most of my friends and family were convinced that a big part of me overcoming this health disaster was down to the fact that I had been leading a healthy life before the crisis happened. Yes, it is very true that when it comes to health, there is a lot to gain from exercising, eating well, hydrating yourself and keeping fit as well as staying mentally positive.

At the same time, when things are out of our hands, we are very fortunate that modern medicine is great at dealing with emergencies, and I was very lucky in that sense. It's incredible to think that someone had been in and out of my head and I was still functioning. However, I also knew that there was something bigger than me and all of us, a source from which I was receiving the strength to live through this unimaginable health crisis.

For some reason, there were moments when I felt like I was already healed in spite of the obvious. I was marvelling at the thought of something or someone who had taken over, and divinely orchestrated all these synchronicities in my life.

The next morning, I was supposed to take another MRI as the doctors had prescribed. Riding on those corridors in a wheelchair was pretty much all the fun I was having.

As the wheelchair was rolling down the dark corridors of the hospital, towards the MRI room, I noticed a big window on my left. Out of the corner of my eye, I could catch a glimpse of the blue sky and a few white beautiful small puffy clouds. I turned my head as the sun rays came through, almost smiling at me. That moment my heart melted and I felt this deep longing. I wanted to stop time and just gaze at that frame. I realised I would have given anything just to be outdoors, to breathe the fresh air and see a small piece of the sky. I remembered how long I'd been in the dark rooms of that hospital and how much I'd missed nature. I felt imprisoned somehow.

The escort stopped the wheelchair just a few steps away from that window in front of the scanning room. He left me there, asking me to wait for my turn a few minutes.

As he left, all I wanted was to get up, rush to the window and gaze outside through that glass. Such a simple thing to do and just steps away from me, and yet I was afraid to take them. I didn't feel confident enough and I was scared of losing my balance. That was the reason I was not allowed to walk by myself, without someone to assist me. It was just a few steps to the left, but that meant I had to get up from the chair and it felt like a big chance to take. I thought, "I could do it," but then fear crept in, "What if you get dizzy and fall over?" I feared that I could injure my head, especially since I did not have a flap bone. What a feeling that was; I had never felt so trapped in that way before.

I was desperately waiting for someone to pass by, so that I could ask them to wheel my chair and place it in front of the window. It's funny how we tend to take little things for granted. The fear that I could not take a few steps on my own, almost brought me to tears. My subconscious prayer was answered as a man passed by.

As I was pointing towards the window, I asked him "Please could you just push me in front of that window just for a minute so that I could look outside and see the sky, until I get my turn to the scan room?" He said, "Of course," and helped me there. As I was gazing at the sky, I felt a wave of warmth and healing energy in my heart, as well as the start of a tear in my eyes. It's incredible to see the effect nature has on our wellbeing, and how it speaks directly to our soul without saying a word.

I remembered how much I was missing outdoors: the fresh air, the sun, and life. I felt that life was something out of reach for me; something that I could only watch from the distance, like a movie playing on the screen that you can't be part of. The room at the hospital was dark and depressing. I could feel how much of a difference a good quality sleep and a bit of sunshine would make in the healing process. I knew exactly what I needed and couldn't wait to go home and help my body and soul heal.

They called my name to go in for the scan. I remember all the time that I was inside that noisy tube, securely fastened with my head fixated in this metal head support, I would affirm silently:

"I am healthy. I am free of all infections, all bacteria, all illnesses and diseases. I am healthy; I am free of all infections, all bacteria and all diseases."

The whole 30 minutes while I was inside that MRI machine, while it was bleeping, grinding and hammering, I was repeating this over and over with conviction, and feeling it in my heart as real.

I was particularly happy when my surgeon came to see me the next morning. There were even more good news. She said that the brain scan looked great and that the infection had cleared up. She told me that they were planning to change my antibiotics to something less invasive and, once they saw that it continued to get better, I could go home with instructions on how to administer the rest of the course of medication by myself.

She also briefed me that she would put me in contact with the maxillofacial surgeon that was going to perform the final surgery; that was, to add a titanium plate to replace the missing part of my skull. She reassured me that he was one of the best and I would be in good hands, but warned me that it was going to take a few months before that procedure would happen.

It was so reassuring to see and hear from her. I actually hugged her and told her that she was in my prayers every day and that my heart would forever be grateful to her, because she had saved my life. Sometimes angels take human form. I truly believe that. At the same time, I am aware that as I say this, I am taking the risk that some of you may assume that I may be a bit of a coo-coo head.

The days that followed seemed to have flown by much quicker than before. The antibiotics were replaced with the milder version the next day. The stitches were also removed the day after. There was the same amount of stitches: approximately 46 of them. It was very painful that time around, so much so, that I had to take a good dose of painkillers to keep up with the pain.

I was getting very close to being discharged, and my heart was jumping with joy every time that thought crossed my mind. I knew it was just around the corner.

The course of antibiotics was to be continued for a few more weeks, and that meant I had to have this intravenous medication administered at home. Instead of three times a day, there were only two doses, one every 12 hours. The hospital arranged for me to have a public nurse visiting every day to administer the first dose and then I would have to administer the evening dose by myself.

The protocol allowed for that to be done by the patient at home, provided that I first went through a short induction to demonstrate that I could perform this process well under supervision. One of the many lovely nurses that was looking after me trained me to do it and yes, I passed the test successfully, twice in a row. I'd watched them administering the medication to me so many times, I knew it by heart.

LOVE LETTER

S pending all that time in the hospital, I came to realize something else. Even though I was always teaching everyone about how we should listen to and respect our bodies, this experience taught me so much more about my own body. It gave me the ability to understand and love my body more than ever before.

I was paying more attention to simple things; like moving my legs, my arms and even being able to use the toilet on my own. These are things we all take for granted, but there are times when simple things like these can become impossible. I could not thank the universe enough that I had been given a second chance. I was grateful to wake up and be able to see the world through those eyes. I was thankful that I could eat and brush my teeth on my own.

There were patients in that hospital who were not able to do any of these things by themselves and needed special assistance with everything. Sometimes we need reminders and life is great at doing that for us.

My heart was filled with compassion and love for my body every time I tried to understand in my own little brain how I had managed to pull through this one. I couldn't stop thinking what a turmoil and what a fight it must have put up for me. After two brain surgeries, I was still able to do all these things on my own. This was the work of the great intelligence that resides in every cell of our body. Our body is the most supreme creation in this universe. There is nothing else in the world that can match it. I was convinced.

From that day onward, I always thanked my body every night and sent love to every cell. I expressed my gratitude for the magical healing that it did for me. It's a wonderful awareness to have as well as a self-care gesture you can practice every day. Here is a letter I wrote in my journal, which I would love to share with you at this point:

My beautiful dear body

I remember all those times you worked so hard to help me run, lift weights, and perform limitless hours of physical activities.

I never really took the time to thank you for any of that and may have even pushed you and taken you for granted. Who would have thought that, after all that happened, you would have to go through so much more?

It's been more than I ever could have imagined possible for you to handle. I never realised how much you did for me, until I was struggling to walk alone, and shower by myself.

I am sorry that you had to go through all the pain of surgeries, all the needles and the chemicals.

Yet, who would have known that, even after this incredible burden you carried for me, you pulled out your most marvelous tricks and got me back on my feet again. Thank you for your love and light that lives in every particle of my being.

I sometimes wish that I had done better for you. At times, I've even blamed myself that I may have brought this onto you.

I promise that I'll remember to thank you every day for everything you do for me.

I promise that I will return the love you showed me all these years, by being kind to you and feeding you nourishing foods and beautiful thoughts and feelings.

I am sorry for the pain I have caused you. I didn't mean for any of this to happen. Please forgive me. I love you.

Mari

A NEW LIFE

On the morning of 21st of November 2019, I woke up knowing that, by that night fall I would be sleeping in my own bed. I was the happiest I'd been in a long time. The nurse handed over a "wagon" of medical equipment including the antibiotics that I was supposed to continue taking over the next four weeks. My sister and my mum came for me that day. We packed everything in five or six bags and headed home.

This time, we went back to my place by the docks. It truly felt like a dream when I first stepped foot in after such a long time. I adored that place, it was so peaceful. The living room was bright, with big windows and a great view over the docks. You could literally see a complete frame of nature without even going outside, just by sitting on the couch. The sky, the blue water, birds and trees all in one view: it was exactly what I needed to see after all the darkness of the hospital. What a lovely, soothing feeling it was.

My flatmate welcomed me with balloons and flowers that filled the living room with a beautiful energy. My middle sister and brother-in-law were also there. They had come back from Sweden to see me after the surgery again. My space was filled with people I loved. It felt so wonderful to be back in a place I could call home.

Needless to say, that the first thing I was looking forward to, was a nice long bath. My mum helped me with that. The PICC line insertion and my swollen head was preventing me from fully enjoying it to be completely honest, as I was being very cautious and always in super slow motion. The nurses advised me to wrap some plastic film around my arm to prevent the dressing from getting wet, and I was also extremely careful not to hit or accidentally wash the wound. Despite all of that, it felt wonderful to have the comfort of my own clean home. It was such a delight.

Later on, we sat together in the living room, had dinner and were just enjoying each other's company. As I rested in my favourite chair by the window, noticing the beautiful, calming view of the water, trees, birds, and people walking slowly by the riverside, I could finally feel my body unwind.

I was feeling tired, but hearing my family chatting in the background and gently giggling brought me a sense of comfort and reassurance. I was finally safe at home, surrounded by loved ones.

Sleeping in my bed was another thing I was longing for. I could still only sleep reclined on two soft pillows. My head was very swollen from all the inflammation and I could not even consider turning on my right side. I didn't have much choice with the sleeping position, but it was nonetheless great to nap in my own bed and to wake up rested and more energised the next day.

In the mornings, my mum would make me breakfast then we'd both sit in the living room, spending most of the day together. She was usually crocheting and I was sometimes sleeping and other times just looking outside the window. Sometimes we would chat and other times just be around each other without talking. Either way, it always felt comforting and never strange, even if we weren't talking.

We designated the whole chest of drawers in the living room to organise all the medication, syringes, and everything that was necessary for the next four weeks. All three big long drawers were full of stuff like saline water bags, antibiotic bottles, plastic syringes, needles, alcohol wipes, flushing syringes, medical gloves, and I'm sure there were more things that I may be missing right now.

The community nurse would come early in the day. While she was preparing and administering my drip of antibiotics every morning, I would sit by the window, watching people passing by. I was longing for a day when I could go back to a normal life and just be out there on my own as well with kids and dogs jumping around everywhere.

In the evening, when it was time for the other dose, my mum would help me. We'd set out a big tray and then sterilize and arrange all the instruments and gadgets carefully, wearing our medical gloves and making sure that everything was clean and disinfected. I remember my flatmate teasing me and calling me Dr Mari.

The recovery process was both a physical and mental challenge. Every day becomes a marathon when you can barely move around and function the way you are used to. The first two weeks I was feeling weak and a bit dizzy at times with all the antibiotics and everything that was going on.

Mentally and emotionally, it was hard to see my head swollen out of proportion every time I looked in the mirror. The doctors said it would take a long time. I could not tell if it had changed at all, so I began to measure it every day. There was only one way that I could think of. I would take a selfie, from a particular spot every day, just to be able to compare them at some point.

As a fitness coach, I always use to advise my clients to monitor their progress. Sometimes you can't tell whether you are making any progress, and the best way to go about it is to have some sort of monitoring process. Taking a selfie, a day, worked well for me.

I was beginning to see improvement, but some days would be better than others. Some days I could prepare my own simple breakfast, and other days I would find it harder. Some days I would feel strong enough to cook my lunch, but other days not so well. Some days I felt like I was more alert, other days more lethargic. I wanted to start reading but I could not concentrate on reading more than a couple of pages. I could watch some TV, but sometimes it felt a bit overwhelming.

The most comfortable, was resting in a quiet environment. Up to that point, my overall strength was up and down, and that incongruence made me have some doubts. I knew I was a long way to recovery, but I wanted to feel a bit more stable. I knew that once my energy was steady for a few days in a row, then that would be a sign of restored balance for my body.

One day I decided to mention this to one of the nurses; she suggested that I might be anaemic as this can happen with serious surgery, especially two in a row. I was looking forward to finishing the antibiotics on the 16th of December.

By the end of November, I could see that the swelling was definitely retracting. However, something very strange happened. I was monitoring my temperature and taking notes. One day, it was a Friday morning, I noticed my temperature was a bit over 37. I was feeling well so I wasn't worried. I thought to myself, "I'm on antibiotics; there is no way that I would have caught anything during this time". I was also isolated at home.

The next day on a Saturday, I took my temperature again and noticed that it had gone up. It was almost 38. This was happening in the evening around 6 pm. I began to worry a bit so I decided to call someone from the ward at the Kings College Hospital to tell them what was going on and see what they suggested.

I got through and managed to speak with one of the lovely nurses that knew me well.

She suggested that I monitor it and take some paracetamol and if it didn't drop, that I should go to the emergency department.

That night my temperature went up again and I could feel every second of it. It went just a bit above 38, but then, an hour later, it was back to normal. I had been ready to go to the A&E, but I was feeling better already and the temperature kept falling back. To be honest I wasn't up to waiting for hours in the hospital and didn't want to risk exposing myself to even more threats.

That evening my son came to visit; he was a bit worried about the temperature but he was also pleased that, whatever it was, my body was reacting well and raising its temperature as a response to a threat. That was a great sign that my immune system was working well.

He suggested that I go to the emergency and check that out. I didn't go that night but I went the day after. During that night, however, I experienced a sharp pain around my ribcage, both front and back. It was strong enough that I had to take painkillers for it. I couldn't get up or lie flat without feeling that sharp pain. It was very strange.

The next day, after the nurse came in the morning to administer my antibiotics, we took a cab and went to the emergency department at Kings College Hospital. My flatmate came with me as my mum was waiting home for us. We waited for hours there, as expected.

Every time a doctor came into the waiting area with a piece of paper looking around the room, my heart would jump as I thought they were going to call my name. Finally, after a very long wait, a young bearded junior doctor showed up and said my name aloud.

He apologised for the long wait and guided me to a small room where he asked me to sit comfortably. He began to ask me about how I was feeling and what had happened. He seemed knowledgeable and he was really listening to every detail. It reassured me when I saw that he was very clear and specific explaining what tests were going to be performed and why.

I was concerned about the fact that I needed my second dose of medication and I didn't want to miss that. He promised that he would arrange for me to have that in the hospital, as soon as he had drawn some blood for tests first. I agreed and thanked him.

He asked me to lie down and began to examine me. He assessed my head first and said it looked good, like it was healing well. Then he also examined my abdominal area explaining, that the fact that the tummy was soft, was a good sign.

When he took some blood, that's when I knew he was an angel. He must have been young enough to be my son. He had angelic features: tall, handsome, blond with blue eyes plus combined with a very calming and reassuring voice. But more than that, when he took my blood, I tell you, I did not even feel the pinch. His hands were so light, it was incredible. When he said, "OK we're done," I was totally confused, as did not even know that he had already started. The reason I say this, is simply because I've never liked needles; but since I had to be pinched countless times to that day, I guess I had became "the toughest audience" at assessing who was naturally gifted for this medical procedure.

Apart from the blood the tests, they also took an X-ray of my chest. As I was waiting for the results, the clock in the waiting room showed that it was time for the second dose of the daily antibiotic. As promised, he arranged that. I laid there plugged in with the antibiotics, while my flatmate kept me company. It was so nice of her to be there for me. All this time, she had never even showed the slightest sign of tiredness or boredom, even though she was there with me for so many hours. I truly appreciated her and the patience she had shown and I thanked her for that.

By the time the antibiotics were inside my body, about 30 minutes later, the results of the tests came back. I was feeling positive for some reason and that was indeed confirmed by the good news. The blood tests were clear; there was nothing concerning. There was a small mark-up for inflammation but it was normal since I had swelling from the brain surgery. The X-rays for the thoracic were clean. The doctor mentioned that there was a thin white line in the corner of my right lung, but after he consulted with his team, they did not find that significant enough to be the cause of anything. He did suggest that I should have another X-ray in the future just to make sure there was no change there. This was clearly not related to the surgery. It may sound crazy, but I felt lighter.

They were intrigued, as they still could not find the reason for the previous increase in body temperature, and the pain I was experiencing around my thoracic area at night. They asked me to wait a bit longer so that they could have a chat with a gallbladder specialist. They thought that it could be something to do with that, since it was the only thing left to examine on the right side of my body that could have caused me that kind of pain.

Finally, the expert came and examined me. He explained that sometimes, when you are over 40 and female, if you have gallstones, it is possible that they may cause some pain when they pass through the tubes. I told him that I have never been examined for gallbladder stones, so he suggested to have a test and see if that is the cause.

He seemed to know what he was talking about and to be truthful, when he explained the pain sensations that it can cause and where, it was exactly the kind of pain I was having.

An ultrasound confirmed that I had such gallstones. Nevertheless, it was not necessarily the cause of the pains that I was having. Many people have gall bladder stones, and may not even know about it, as they usually have no major side effects. Later I found out that my mother has this as well and she never had any issues from what she explained later on. How peculiar!

The humorous thing about this whole situation was that, while I was on the go the whole day, taking tests and patiently waiting for a verdict, I had no pain or discomfort at all. Not just that, but I was feeling incredibly good physically. In addition, there was no sign of temperature or pain.

At home, my mom was getting worried despite the fact that I was constantly keeping her up to date. No wonder; it was already dark outside and we had been out the whole day. When we arrived home, she was waiting for us with warm soup that she had prepared while she was waiting. It reminded me of the old times back home, when I would come back late from school, to find her waiting for me with supper.

The first thing I did when I arrived home was to change all my clothes, put them straight into the washing and have a shower. Needless to say, since I was back from the second surgery, I was extra cautious not to catch another infection, or any kind of bug for that matter. My immunity was much lower than usual, and I was already traumatically marked by the experience. When my family or friends came to visit, they would always wash their hands and sanitize before coming in contact with me.

We sat down and enjoyed the heart-warming food my mum had made. It is very true when they say, that there is no better food than the meals your mum makes for you. I guess it has to do with the love ingredient.

I continued to feel well and the temperature and pain never came back. To be completely honest, to this day, I am still not sure what caused the pain and temperature I had those few days. All I know is that it magically disappeared.

It was almost midnight, way past my bedtime, and I was ready to rest my body after the long day. I felt so much gratitude that all my results had come back clean, that everything was well and, most importantly, I was feeling great.

As I lit a candle in my little sacred corner, tears of gratitude slid down my face. I turned my head and looked up to a canvas that was hanging on my wall. It was the same image I had on my phone as a screensaver: my guardian Angel Raphael. I had wanted a full-size version since I was in the hospital and was looking at my phone screen every evening, praying and asking him for help. Soon after I was discharged, I asked my mum to help me get that printed.

With a burning heart, I asked him for a smooth journey to recovery. I was tired of hospitals, needles and pain. That day I realised that I had too much of it, and could not take it anymore. I just wanted to be free of discomfort, worries and doubts. I felt a sense of reassurance within my deep faith, and I thanked the universe for giving me all of that already. I slept like a baby afterwards.

From that day onwards, things began to get better and better. I began to feel a bit more like myself every day. I could feel myself getting stronger and steadier. The swelling was lessening day by day. It didn't look like and elephant head anymore.

When the sun was out and shining, I would go out for a breath of fresh air on long walks with my mom. It was always refreshing and it felt good to be able to go outside and walk around my beautiful neighbourhood. That place had such a pleasant healing energy. I guess it's the combination of all the nature elements that makes it distinctively beautiful: water, trees, blue sky and birds squeaking and flying over the water.

I remember holding my mums' arm while I was walking by her side. I was feeling insecure about walking on my own for more than a few steps when I was outside. I still felt like I needed support.

She was happy to walk with me, and we both enjoyed that time together. I was feeling revitalised each time after we'd get back from being out in nature. She would go back to crocheting my rainbow blanket that she intended to have ready by Christmas. I would lie down to rest for a while and then read a bit more every day.

I have to admit that, even though most of the time I had a positive attitude towards everything that happened and never felt the need to complain, there were also naturally, many low moments when my mind was filled with doubt and fears, remembering the past nightmare.

I was reminded that we cannot take anything for granted, and you cannot know what will happen tomorrow. I guess, remembering how I got the infection and the moment when I felt the wet texture of the pus on my fingertips, I realised, that moment had a deep traumatic effect on me.

Even months after that incident, there were many times when I had a physical sensation that something was dripping off my face. I would immediately have the instinct to check if my face was dry and reach out to touch that exact spot where I had felt that terrifying fluid back then. Of course, this was just an illusion. It never happened. It was just an imaginary scar, a mental trauma.

There were moments when I was worried that something might happen again, and I would have to go back to the hospital. One time I thought, "What if I don't get to be with my family for Christmas?"

Because of this thought, I had the impulse to buy their presents way in advance just to make sure. Of course, I did all of this online. I even wrapped everything and put them under the Christmas tree, on the second day of December, way early! Fear can make you do crazy things sometimes!

Therefore, yes, going through traumatic experiences can scar you very deeply. But what I have learnt, is that they can only scar you as deep as you allow them to. With faith, belief and a positive mental attitude, anything is possible. The tools are always available both within us and outside ourselves, through people that can help you if you need it. You can take charge of your thoughts and help your body and brain recover from anything as long as you are willing to.

There are always ups and downs, and sometimes even hills and mountains to cross, but I've learnt that you have to walk up to them with faith, knowing that there is a reason they are there, in your way.

What if they are there, not to bring you down, but to help you discover your greatest strengths? What if you made a bet with yourself in a past life that you will make it through and you knew that you would? What if your higher self is cheering you along the way?

FREEDOM

I was counting down the last ten days to the 16th of December when I was finally going to have the follow up and final tests. In the meantime, the struggle was real; I was beginning to get so tired of that wire in my arm and of all the antibiotics, I just could not wait for it to be over. When that day came, it was magical. I can still remember how smoothly everything went.

Having talked with the oncology team the day before, I went to see the specialists from the team that had operated on me.

I had to take some blood tests, then a CT scan of my head and then would have to wait until the specialist was free to see me. She told me that it was going to be a bit of a wait, but I did not mind at all.

I did the blood tests in less than 10 minutes including the wait. That was much faster than expected so I was ahead of the schedule. It was too early for the scan and I thought I had to wait for another 45 minutes to get that done. However, I took a chance and asked if they could see me earlier. Luckily, they were happy to, so I walked straight in. They were very nice and accommodating. CT scans are much faster than the MRIs so it only took 10 minutes. By now, you can probably guess what I was doing during the scan. Yes, that's right! I was repeating my affirmations silently in my head over and over.

I am healthy, I am free of all infections, all inflammations, or diseases.

The catch was that, if the infection wasn't completely gone, then I would have to continue with antibiotics and that meant I could not yet get rid of that thing in my arm, which was becoming more and more uncomfortable. The good thing was that the swelling was almost gone.

It didn't take more than 10 minutes in the waiting area before I was called in to see the specialist. I did not know who was going to see me, but I was hoping that it was going to be Anna, the neurosurgeon lady. It wasn't her, but I was happy to hear that the head scan looked beautiful, in the exact words of the specialist, and the blood test results were normal. I almost jumped with joy when he told me that I could discontinue the antibiotics and have the PICC line removed.

Before I left, I asked him to have a look at my red blood cell count, as I was feeling a bit weak at times. He told me my blood count was 80, which was quite low. It wasn't surprising after two brain surgeries in a row. I knew that it usually takes around three months for the red blood cells to regenerate naturally, but he suggested that I get some iron supplement for a while, which I did later on.

Half an hour later, I was sitting in the same room where I had the procedure to insert the PICC line a few weeks back. It was the same guy that had done the process in the first place. When he removed it, I was shocked once again, seeing him holding this long thin tube of approximately 45 cm. It was hard to believe that it had been in my body the whole time. I guess the human body is a friendly environment after all. There was literally a tiny hole in my arm where the tube was inserted. He asked me to keep the wound dry for 24 hours. I felt so happy.

Just as I was walking out of the hospital, by the exit door, guess who I bumped into? It was Anna, the lady who had literally gone into my head twice and saved my life. She was happy to see me too; the first thing she said was, "I saw your scan earlier, it looked amazing". We chatted a bit more, then we wished each other a Merry Christmas and hugged. It was almost like magic, as I was really hoping to see her that day and there she was!

She was on her way home but she had been stopped by a colleague just as she was exiting the hospital. Imagine the "orchestration". It meant a lot to me to see her that day. It felt reassuring and like a happy end to another chapter.

Riding the taxi on the way home with my flatmate, who had been with me the whole time, I felt like I was tasting the sweetness of freedom once again.

I was excited for Christmas because my family planned to spend it at my place. I was really looking forward to enjoy the holidays, without needles, without medication, and just to be able to move around freely and independently. It was very hard for my body and I felt invaded and restricted all that time. But not anymore!

It was indeed a full house and a wonderful day. We exchanged presents, we had a wonderful meal, and everything was just delightful. We called my dad who was back home in Romania. He showed us all the delicious traditional food he had prepared all by himself. I felt sad that he was alone and couldn't be there with us, but I knew he could not travel at the time as he was having some health issues.

That evening, as I was just sitting there, watching us all together, I felt so much appreciation that I was alive that Christmas. I could not imagine what this would have been like for them, if things hadn't unfolded so well.

After Christmas I tried to convince my mum to go back home to my dad. He had been alone for almost two months, and he wasn't perfectly healthy either. It was a big deal for him to be looking after himself for almost two months. I know he did it all for me. He wanted my mum to be with me until I did not need her assistance anymore, but I knew he also needed help. I didn't want him to be by himself for the New Year as well, so I eventually convinced her.

To be honest, it wasn't that hard to reassure her. The fact was, that I was getting much better and I could do a lot more on my own. She could see that for herself. She was happy that I could bathe alone, make my own meals and even clean a bit around the house.

That stable condition that I had been waiting for, to feel energised and balanced for many days in a row, finally came to be a reality.

She only agreed to go back for a little while, but she wanted to come back as soon as we had a date for the next surgery. I had an appointment with the maxillofacial surgeon that was going to perform this procedure on the 10th of January 2020. I was looking forward to that.

We finally got her on a plane back home on the 28th of December. It was hard to see her go. I was already missing her just as I watched her leaving. All the time we had spent together, even in those circumstances, had brought us closer. I remember one day my flatmate saying, "I don't know how you can spend so much time with your mum without fighting or arguing". That made me smile. I told her, we did have our serious conversations from time to time, just like any family members would, but we didn't usually argue even if the subject of the discussion was sensitive.

The next day, home wasn't the same without her. I could almost still see her knitting my huge rainbow blanket by the window, which was now covering my bed. It looked beautiful and brought so much vibrancy to the space. I remembered how she used to massage my feet, my arms and my legs just to make me feel comfortable enough to get some rest. I remembered how she'd kiss my hands and how I could feel her love wrapping me and healing me instantly. There is nothing more powerful than the love of a mother. I still could not imagine how hard it must have been for her to see her child going through such a challenge.

I was happy to hear that she got back home safely and was reunited with my dad. As I sat in her chair by the window, gazing outside, I could see the wind blowing about the trees and the birds flying around agitated and squeaking almost like announcing the rain. Heavy raindrops followed shortly after. Everyone who was out started to look for shelter and going at a faster pace. It made me realise something.

When the weather is sunny, the sky is blue and sun shines, everyone and everything is outside. Every being enjoys the nature and the lovely climate. Everything is relaxed and expanding.

When the rain starts to fall and wind is blowing, everyone is looking for shelter, seeking the comfort of indoors and watching the cold weather through the window, while sipping at a warm cup of tea at home. It starts to feel like everything is retreating, just the opposite of expansion.

It is the same for us: when everything is fine in life, and things are going well, we are happy. We enjoy life and everything around us. We look outward for new pleasant experiences.

But when things get tough, or we are faced with a crisis, we look for refuge; we turn inwards, to look for shelter within ourselves, to see what matters the most and makes us feel happy. We look for something to fill that cup of tea to feel warm and safe while the rain falls outside.

I understood that crisis brings us closer to ourselves. It opens us up from the inside and makes us more appreciative of things and people we otherwise take for granted. We especially do that with the people we love most: our family.

Before my mum left, I had written a letter to both her and my dad and asked her to read it when she gets home. I just wanted to thank them for everything they had done for me all this time, to say how grateful I was for all the efforts and sacrifices they had made for me and to remind them how much I love them.

I don't remember being so outwards about my feelings with them before this. It was a great way to finally open up and tell the people I love how much I appreciate them. Storms will change us from the inside out, bring families even closer, and heal the most hidden parts of ourselves.

YEAR END CONTEMPLATIONS

B efore I knew it, there I was on 31st of December 2019, after an incredible emotional and physical rollercoaster of a year.

I sat down by my favourite spot by the window, thinking how unbelievable this year had been.

"What lessons have I learned this year?" I thought to myself, "If I am still here after all of this, there has to be a reason for it. There has to be more to this than just my own life. I am obviously not done yet."

Looking back, it all seemed surreal. First, there was the chickenpox in early February. It continued with ovarian cysts, unbearable migraines every month, surgery to remove the cysts in July, followed by the emotional trauma with the kidney biopsy in August. As if that was not enough, by November, I wrapped it up with two brain surgeries. Is your mind blown or is it just me? I feel breathless just writing this. What a ride!

Flashes of memory were playing in my mind. Looking back at it, I was still wondering where I had found the strength to go through it all.

It is true that strength is like an armour we all have within and we pull it out whenever life calls us to "battle". In my case, the armour was made of much more than inner strength. It was plated with the love and support of my family and friends. The love and support of family doesn't just make you feel worthy and loved; it also gives you the power to cope with whatever is in front of you.

That year I've learnt that without them, I would not have been where I was at that moment. They had been my rock to lean on, the reassuring hand that held mine. At the core of everything, my faith in God kept me going despite all adversities, and it made that heavy load feel lighter.

I've learnt that life can radically shift you in many directions without any warning. But even when that happens, it's a temporary situation. It's not forever. It will change. You need to adjust your sails. Most of the times you need to be flexible and allowing and other times you may need to pull out your best armour and see yourself to the end of it.

My greatest lesson for that year was clear. As much as we'd like to believe that we control every outcome in life, we are often shown that there are other forces in nature that can't be controlled. If we'd only open our minds and hearts more, like a wise sailor, we'll instinctively know to adjust our sails and go with the wind when storms are unfolding.

I've learnt that stormy days are difficult, but they won't last forever. In fact, everything is always changing. Nothing is forever. Life itself is not forever. Only love is eternal. Spending so many days in the hospital that year, I understood what second chances and rebirth meant. I learnt what surrendering truly means. I learnt blind faith. I realised how lucky and blessed I was to still be alive. Every day we open our eyes, we have a bright new chance to honour and appreciate every moment of our life. There is so much gold in these experiences.

I spent that New Year's Eve with my son and his fiancée. They came by, and we cooked together and bonded. We chatted about the incredible year and also brighter future. We talked about their wedding plans for May 2021 and got even more excited about that. The fact that it was taking place in Bali, added another dose of excitement to it. I'd never been to Bali before and there was certainly going to be an extended holiday after the wedding.

NEW YEAR NEW HOPE

The New Year brought a sense of new hope to everyone. I was waking up feeling better and stronger day by day. London didn't really have much of a winter and some days were so beautiful and sunny, they were just calling me outside.

I will never forget the first time I went outdoors by myself after the surgery. One morning, I woke up and looked out the window. It was such a glorious sunny morning. I thought, "I wish I could go out…" The wisdom of the willow tree whispered in my heart, *"Don't be afraid, you can do it!"* Instantly, I took a brave decision. I wrapped up well and went outside to enjoy the sunshine. I told my flatmate I'd do it alone this time; she smiled and said, "OK, I'll be watching you from the window."

On my way out, going down the stairs carefully and in slow motion, I was telling myself "Easy does it, step by step". I was holding onto the railing and being extra cautious. The closer I was to the door, the more my excitement was building up. This was about to be the first time I had actually been outside on my own since before the 9th of October 2019. That was more than three months earlier. I was smiling at the idea that such a small, "insignificant thing" was making me feel so joyful. But of course, it was! It was my freedom.

A few steps and a turn around the corner, and there I was, all on my own, standing free and independent in nature again. The feeling of the warm rays on my forehead felt like the welcoming, loving kisses of my grandparents from heaven. The fresh air was filling my lungs with life and my whole body was vibrating with it. It felt so liberating. I couldn't wait to get closer to the water and watch the birds flying around.

As I was gently walking through the rays, I could see the infinite reflection of the sun in the ripples of the water. It looked like a million diamonds shining from beneath.

There weren't many people around, so I kept walking very slowly and cautiously alongside the river. The more steps I took on my own, the more confident I felt and the more my heart smiled; and my face could not hide that feeling. At one point, I just wanted to open my arms, look up and cry tears of happiness.

We take so many things for granted and this was one of them. A simple thing like this, to walk independently on your own, and yet a little while ago, I had not been able to do it.

There was no fear anymore. I felt calm and so immersed in nature. All my senses were instantly alert but relaxed at the same time. My heart was overflowing with joy, and appreciation of the gravity that was making me feel more and more confident with each step.

As I kept walking, I noticed that the sparkles on water were following me. No matter how far along I went, whenever I looked over my shoulder, the sparkling diamonds were right there on the surface of the water. I smiled and stopped for a while to admire them a bit more. I am mesmerised by this simple phenomenon of nature every single time I happen to witness it. I could stare at it forever.

As I was losing myself in the beauty of this wonder of nature, a series of contemplations flew through me, almost like a download of information.

The light never lives us. It's always with us. The current and the ripples are inextricably connected with the light. If there were no ripples, we would only see a single reflection of the sun in the water. Just like a mirror that never changes.

But what's the fun in being omnipotent, omniscient and omnipresent if you're alone forever? So, the universe created the current and the ripples so that the sun could see infinite versions of its magnificent beauty. Each reflection that seems to shine like a diamond in the water is just another beautiful unique form of the sun itself.

Humans are beings of light too, created from a single source of divine energy. We are just like the reflections of the sun in the water created by the ripples. We are like those little diamonds in the water. Even though we think we are separated from each other, we are reflections of the same thing. We may seem different with different shapes, sizes and appearance on the outside; but on the inside, at the core of our existence, we are all identical. In truth, we are never alone, but always inevitably connected with each other and with the powerful source that creates life.

I sat down on a bench and allowed that to sink in for a while.

Talking about first times after the surgery, I just remembered of another important moment for me: the first time I crossed the road. Yes, I know, it sounds silly when you think about the simplicity of it, but that was a big deal for me at the time. I guess it's all about the mental blocks, fears and insecurities that take over after a traumatic experience.

One day, when the weather was beautiful, I decided to go to the park. This involved a fair bit of walking and a main road to cross. I recall stopping at the crossing and patiently waiting for the light to turn green, as well as making sure that all the cars have stopped before I took the first step. My confidence was so boosted when I got to the other side. I was literally smiling at myself. It was like the first time I crossed the road without my parents; only now, I was in my 40s. Imagine that!

When I walked into the park, it seemed like I had stepped into heaven. The energy of the old trees was incredibly calming, and the rays of sun made the grass and the green crowns of the trees look so heavenly. The warm sun was kissing my face and I was just standing there, with my eyes closed, smiling at the sky wanting to take it all in. Nature never seemed more beautiful.

This park was very familiar to me. I've been there many times in the past. I couldn't stop feeling thankful that I was still around to enjoy that day. I was breathing all the air my lungs could hold, and was ecstatic that I could walk on my own and be there.

As I was walking through the alleys, memories were rushing back to me. I could see flashbacks of myself running there not long ago. I could see boot camp classes on Sunday mornings, people sweating, laughing and having fun. It was like scenes from the movie of my life playing before me.

I remembered what a big part fitness had always played in my life; so big, it had almost defined me. When fitness and working out is such a big slice of your life, it becomes a major habit and you think that is your identity and who you are. It had been hard when it was taken away.

I had thought my purpose in life was to help people get back in shape, and win back their health and confidence. I guess doing that had helped me get mine too. Now, I did not see where my life was heading in terms of career. I wasn't sure if I could ever be as physically strong as I had been prior to the surgery. There were moments when I had doubted my own reason for existence. I knew there had to be more to my life; I just couldn't imagine what that was yet.

In that second, I caught myself riding waves of past memories. These had been great times, which had brought beautiful feelings. However, at the same time, there was a taste of nostalgia and even a bit of tension in the thoughts, because I didn't have the faintest idea what the future would bring. I wasn't ready to think too far ahead. In addition, it was beginning to taint my beautiful *first time in the park experience.*

I realised that I needed to fully shift my energy towards my physical, emotional and mental healing. I knew that, when the time was right, I would cross the next bridge as well. There was a long journey ahead before that bridge. All I knew for sure was that I was happy and grateful to be alive and to experience that moment of time. I left the old memories behind, continued my walk in the park and enjoyed the rest of that stroll.

Before I knew it, January 10th came.

I was so excited to meet Mr Bentley, the maxillofacial expert who was going to perform this final procedure for me. I had heard so much about how great he was in his field, and I was counting on that. I also wanted a bit of reassurance and someone to have a look at the wound and let me know how it was doing. It was healing well, but some bits of dead skin and hair were stuck together, forming something that looked yucky and scabby.

His assistant pre-assessed me and was happy to see that all my motor functions were on point. She was also very impressed with my medical file and the whole situation. She actually said, "Wow I read your medical history. That is quite a story you have there", she said. Funnily enough, I was considering writing this book at that time, but I wasn't quite ready, as my ability to focus was still weak, but the messages were coming through already.

When the expert took over and began the physical assessment of the wound, I was almost shocked to see how he pressed against my flapless head without any reluctance. He told me that next time I washed my hair, I should rub that part of my scalp with my fingertips using some oil and then wash it with shampoo. He literally took my four fingers and showed me how much pressure I could apply when I was doing that. I thought he was joking, but he was serious. He was pushing against it, almost as if it was nothing.

The truth is that, until that time, I had never dared and had been scared to touch the wound with my fingers the way that he did. As a result, my hair was growing, which was a great thing, but there was a lot of dead skin and the hair was literally stuck together. It looked something like too much hair gel stuck to my hair.

He also took a pair of tweezers and removed the last couple of scabs that were forming around the wound. I was in a bit of panic and shock when he showed me the scabs he had pulled out and my blood on his surgical gloves. He made it all look like it wasn't a big deal at all. I guess because it wasn't really. Then, he called his assistant and asked her to maintain pressure on the wound until the blood stopped. Despite the obvious distress, at the same time, I felt some reassurance and realised that things were much better than I thought, and that I was not quite as fragile as I had imagined.

He then went and explained in detail the whole process of the planned surgery. The plan was to add a titanium plate to replace the missing part of the skull. The whole titanium piece was to be built by a robot using a computer image of my skull. How cool, I thought to myself. "It would be fixed into the skull with multiple screws", he continued. "Wow, it sounds like

I'm on my way to become a bionic woman", I said out loud. He laughed, and he then continued telling me that I would have a general anaesthetic and a tube drain for a couple of days that would allow the excessive blood to drain out after the operation.

All of it sounded insane to me, but it was a real thing. He said that I would only be there for a few days and that, due to the infection history, he would also administer some antibiotics.

Of course, as every medical surgeon does, he also highlighted some of the things that could go wrong, which you already know by now. At the same time, he was very reassuring and somehow made me feel safe and excited to go ahead with it. He instructed the assistant to book me a day for the procedure to be done around April, May 2020 and he left saying that we'd meet again soon. I had been hoping to have it sooner than that, but there was nothing I could do about it. His assistant provisionally booked a spot for the surgery, for the 14th of April and said that they would confirm it in the meantime. I left there feeling excited and looking forward to that day.

When I got back home, I started to clean the wound just as the doctor had advised. I was amazed by the amount of dead skin and hair I had removed from the area. It was quite messy and yucky. I felt a bit triggered by the fact that no one else had told me how to look after the wound before. However, as soon as I had done it, I could see how my skin was breathing and I felt much better. I knew that it was very important for the wound to be healed and that meant, my skin and hair had to be in the best condition possible by the time of the surgery.

I had a soft new toothbrush with natural hairs and I used that to clean the area. It worked so well. As proof, I started to grow new little hairs soon after that. My scalp was breathing again and it was healing very well.

A couple of weeks later I received a written confirmation for the surgery on the 14th of April 2020 and a phone call to confirm a pre-op full assessment on the 23rd of March.

I began to prepare myself mentally for the next surgery and also for another three months of waiting, plus, being safe and avoiding crowded places. This was of course, to make sure that I get myself in the best condition possible. Except for the days that I would go out in nature, and for the appointments that I had to attend, I wasn't really going anywhere. I was very much in isolation.

During this time, I continued to treat my body the best way I knew. I was eating mostly all organic and I eliminated all foods that I knew were not great for someone on their way to healing. I wasn't eating any simple sugars like cakes, biscuits or other sweet treats. I was also off coffee completely and stayed away from dairy with a few minor exceptions. I had made a promise to my body and I was all in to keep it.

I began to feel better and better. My mental focus was improving. I was able to read more than two pages at one time, and was journaling every day. Physically I felt stronger and I started to move my body more than I had been able to, in a long time.

I remember waking up to a glorious Sunday morning on the 1st of March 2020. Somehow, a sunny morning always puts a smile on my face. I had just about finished my morning rituals when I heard the sound of loud music playing outside. I was thinking to myself, "that's a bit too early for a party". It sounded like a big celebration, as I could hear someone speaking loudly through a microphone. I opened the windows in the living room by the riverside and enjoyed the sun. I stayed there for a bit, just taking it all in. The sparkles in the water were calling me to go outside. It was such a lovely day. I said to myself, "let me open the windows in my room to allow some of this beautiful freshness in there as well".

As I was making my way to my room which was facing the opposite side of the water, the sound of the music and cheering got louder and louder. When I pulled the curtains and opened the windows, I realised that the whole party was right there under my nose. It was a half marathon day event in London and people were cheering the runners as they passed by.

There were so many of them and they kept coming for more than an hour. I just stood there watching them, in their shorts and fitness gears. The colorful sight was so pleasing for me to see. They were so lucky to have such a beautiful day on which to run. As I was standing by my bedroom window watching them, a bigger smile took over my face and my heart cheered for them as well. I could hear familiar tunes playing along with the clapping. The sun was shining on them, almost like spotlights on a stage. They looked so free and happy.

That instant, a rush of memories and emotions came over me. I felt what they were feeling. I remembered how it felt to run, to be outdoors and to feel that freedom and the nirvana from all the happy hormones. I remembered how much I had missed exercising and that feeling that comes with it. I felt like a child who wants so badly to barge out the door, but she's been grounded. A few tears of nostalgia slid down my face.

I was thinking of the future and the day that I'd feel strong again to resume physical activity. When I was watching all these people running right under my window that day, I would have given anything to feel that rush and sweat from exercise again.

Despite that, I continued to stay positive and focused to build my strength for the upcoming surgery. Physically I was getting better and better. My body was healing so well. Day by day, I was feeling stronger and stronger and I began to walk more and faster every day.

PART THREE

THE LAST MOUNTAIN

THE PANDEMIC

When the rumours first started, it seemed more like fake news, but the reality quickly took over the world. I wasn't watching the news, I never do, but it was all over social media and everyone was talking about it. There was a deadly virus that was taking the lives of many people all over the world.

My flatmate was getting more and more anxious about it. I remember one day her talking about how she wanted to freeze her gym membership. She did not want to risk getting infected. It sounded surreal. At the same time, I was chatting with my sister and my friends as well and I was constantly updated on everything that was happening.

About the same time, my sister was in the process of buying a new home. I was so excited for her and for me as well, as that meant of course, that we could move in together. The new house was almost ready but she was worried that this global situation would get in the way of our plans. It didn't take long before the UK officially declared lockdown and so the nightmare was as real as it could get. The whole world was in lockdown.

As we were all going through massive changes, most people started to panic to the point that all the toilet paper in the superstores was gone. I think that this "toilet paper situation" is one story that will make it to the history books. People were preparing for a long-term lockdown and buying excessive amounts of long-lasting food supplies. Long lines with overloaded trolleys and isles of empty shelves in the big supermarkets was an incredible scene. People panicked so much and wanted to buy everything they could get. The sad part was that elderly people and other fellow humans who could not keep up with the frantic actions of the majority, also needed provisions, but were being left with nothing.

It broke my heart to see pictures and videos all over the media, with old people pushing empty trolleys along the isles with empty shelves. Up to that point, I had been getting my groceries online as I was avoiding crowded places, and I could not carry much weight anyway. It had worked great for me so far, but now, online shopping slots were impossible to find. There was no availability at all for months ahead.

Luckily, a week before they announced it, I managed to get a few on-line slots and had enough water and food for a couple of weeks. However, after that, there was nothing. I could not believe that I was living through such a nightmare.

In addition, people with lower immunity or special health cases like myself, were more prone to being affected by this virus so, I didn't want to risk going out for supplies myself. I was very blessed that I had this one close friend who lived nearby, and always used to call me before he went shopping to ask if I need anything. He knew I was avoiding crowded places and the whole reason for it.

It was very stressful, especially at the beginning, but what worried me the most was that the surgery would get cancelled. It didn't take long, and one day I received a call that confirmed it. Due to the worldwide pandemic, all non-urgent surgical procedures were cancelled until further notice.

When I got off the call, I felt like my wings had dropped to the floor. I could not believe it, I had been just three weeks away from the surgery. It was disheartening because all this time, I had been preparing mentally and physically for that moment, and now there was nothing. The sad part was that I did not even know when it was going to happen at all. I felt like I had been left hanging somewhere in the unknown. I felt even more sad realising that in reality I had already been in "lockdown" since November 2019 and was getting really tired of feeling restricted. Four months later, in March 2020, the whole world had now decided to join me. How bizarre was that?

Even though it was disappointing to hear the news, a part of me had seen it coming. That's why another part felt relieved. I did not feel quite safe having surgery while the whole world was fighting a deadly virus and people were flooding the hospitals, struggling for their lives. It was safer for me to stay at home until the situation changed.

And so, another lesson in patience began. I was faced with another mindset challenge. How could I go on from there? How could I convince myself that this was fine? It had been a tough ride already, but this time it felt like the whole world was in the same boat with me.

Stuck in the flat, without being able to move as much, especially when I was beginning to feel stronger, was frustrating. I was now literally scared to go outside. I was afraid of being in close proximity to people. Who would have thought that, as someone who loves people, I would one day avoid them thinking that they were the "enemy"?

I felt trapped; when I could not take it any longer, I came up with a solution. Since the issue was, not wanting to be in close range to any human, I would wake up at 5 am to go out for a walk. I needed to move my body and get some fresh air. Of course, there was a whole process of covering my face and hands to make sure I was safe and disinfecting everything and washing all my clothes after getting back inside.

Even though I found a way to be outdoors early in the morning and connect with nature, I still did not feel that complete freedom, because I was stressing out every time I saw someone coming in the distance. Despite all that, I was grateful that I could get some fresh air and move my body for half an hour. Also, the sunrises were magnificent.

This continued for a while, but with all the difficulties, I was slowly getting used to it. I learnt to keep my distance from people; I would wave from afar, to say, "Hello" as a sign of saying "It's not you, but the virus I am avoiding". They would wave back and it became kind of a sign language of acknowledgement, compassion and understanding for each other. It made me think even more about freedom and how much we take it for granted sometimes. I was looking forward to a brighter day when these invisible prison bars would be behind us.

It was such a frightening idea to be "invaded" by this threatening virus. I remember that, when the food deliveries came, I literally wiped every single item with alcohol at the door, before even getting it into the kitchen. That was quite a stressful process. For the first time in the history of humanity, people were being taught how to wash their hands and the internet was flooded with such videos.

At the same time, I also had great things to look forward to. My sister was updating me on the new home progress and sending pictures of the house. I was so excited to hear that the house was finished and almost all documents were approved and ready to be signed off, except for one final one. This was the most important, though. The whole deal could still go out the window if this paper wasn't in place.

I began to visualise myself in the new home: being in the garden and the freedom of breathing freely in my own space and all of us hugging each other in joy. I was doing this daily with conviction and feeling.

I remember how extremely happy I was when she called me and said, "It's time we start packing!" The final document was approved, keys were handed over and they officially declared that we could move into our new home anytime: my sister, my nephew and myself. It was a great milestone. In addition, the lease of the place I was living at that time was coming to an end, so it all worked out perfectly.

In the first week of May, while we were still officially in lockdown mode, my sister came and we loaded everything I had, and headed to the new home, just 40 minutes outside London. There were some exceptions to the rule of lockdown, and one of them was moving into a new property. It was magic how everything had been approved and run so smoothly. I felt sad to leave that place and say my goodbyes to my flatmate, as she had been such great support for me. At the same time, I was also excited to move in with family again and be even closer to nature living in a detached, four-bedroom house.

The first few weeks in the new home went by so quickly. There's great excitement that comes with moving into a new place. I remember hanging my Angel canvas on the wall in my bright new room with a view over the back garden, and the feeling of starting a fresh new chapter. There were so many particulars and little things to do. The fact that this was a detached home with a big garden, outside the city made me feel so free and safe. The fresh air and the feeling of freedom helped so much with my healing process. I even planted my own apple tree in the garden. I don't think I'd ever planted a tree before.

Every morning I would water the freshly planted lawn and flowers. I remember chasing the rainbow that was created from the precise conjunction of sunlight and fine water particles coming together. It was so bright and incredibly beautiful to watch. I loved spending time in our big kitchen, cooking lovely meals and baking cakes for my family. This one thing I got from my mum for sure.

The whole vibe was different to the one in the city. It was peaceful, and the forest was just a few minutes around the corner. Spending daily time in the woods contributed to my healing and physical strength a great deal. I was feeling so well. I could sleep normally with no restrictions whatsoever, on both sides and that was such a great feeling. I began to exercise regularly; it was incredible to feel more like myself again.

Time flies so fast and before you know it, I was eating apples from my apple tree; I could not believe it was almost end of August 2020. Even though I could easily get used to that life, and I was beginning to feel balanced and almost "normal" again, I still could not help thinking about the fact that I had one more surgery to go through. I remembered that I was still a long way from full recovery.

MORE MIRACLES

While I was patiently waiting for a word from the hospital about the upcoming surgery, the pandemic situation started to improve. Most countries in the world, with a few exceptions had lifted the lockdown and that was also the case for the UK. Things were getting better and people started to get out more, some even travelling abroad. Despite that, there were times when I felt that I had been left hanging, because I had no news about the surgery. I had no idea of how my healing path would unfold.

That thought sometimes made me feel anxious. The unknown felt uncomfortable. I knew there was nothing I could do, except surrender and wait. I still took some action and made a few calls to my nurse friend who promised to help if she could. I did my best with the whole situation from day one. Some days were easier than others, but I kept my faith and that always lifted my spirit.

I remember one day, scrolling through my photos on my phone as I was clearing some space. There was a picture of an X-ray of my skull with a huge missing part of it. It was a reminder and still surreal, but I had a big hole in my skull. Next to that picture, there was another one of me smiling as if nothing had ever happened, looking so bright and shiny on the outside, you could never tell.

I was reminded that I had been living without that bone flap for ten months; I was in awe of my body and the way that it had just adjusted, not just to keep me alive, but also to support me to be able to do all the things that I was doing.

My mind went back to memories of the storm and, even though some were still vivid, I knew that it was behind me. I felt energised and lively just being able to exercise, cook, read, write, and help around the house. There were even times when I forgot that I'd been through two brain surgeries. How miraculous!

I could smell the roses in my garden, and feel the soft breeze. I could lie in the grass and gaze at the beautiful blue sky until I was lost in it. All my five senses, which allowed me to experience this life, were intact. What a blessing!

I realised that I had this amazing body; a vessel that loved me so much that was willing to keep me alive no matter what. It had a greater purpose; to keep my soul safe and help it to express itself in this human form.

The more I thought about the journey from day one until that moment, the more I realised how magical this was. "I know it isn't me. It can't be just me. There is more to this." As thoughts of how this could have gone wrong and the effect it would have had on my loved ones crossed my mind again, avalanches of emotion began to build up.

I felt the need to put all this behind me, but I couldn't. There was still one more surgery to go and another big mountain to climb. One that I knew nothing about. It was all a mystery. I felt all my emotions turning into warm tears on my cheeks.

I turned to the canvas of my guardian Angel Raphael, which was hanging on my wall. As I looked at it through my tears, I felt a sense of surrender and trust. I said aloud:

You've always been with me and I felt your healing energy wrapped around me so many times. I am so grateful that you are by my side and always keep me safe. I now let go of all my worries and concerns and hand them over to you. I know in my heart that one day soon, you will bring me great news, and I know that it will be the perfect timing.

As I said these words, I felt them deeply sinking in my heart, and a deep sense of peace and calm followed after. I took a deep breath that filled my body with a soothing energy.

Another month of long walks in nature, meditations, reading, reflections and deep inward dives went by quickly. Then, on the 17th of September, my phone rang from an unknown number. My heart skipped a bit, as somehow, I knew it was from the hospital.

My sister was watching me walking back and forward as I was on the call; she figured out what was happening. When I got off the phone, I could not hold back the tears of joy. I had been waiting for this moment so patiently and it had finally arrived. I hugged my sister and she hugged me back as I was crying and smiling sharing the news. To be honest, I had been visualising for weeks the moment when someone would call me with the good news. Yes, this was it. I had a date for the surgery. The 29th of September.

The nurse also informed me of the whole protocol prior to and post-surgery. From that moment until the surgery, I was supposed to be in complete isolation and the same would apply for two weeks post-surgery to avoid the risk of me being contaminated. The pandemic rules were still very strictly in effect in hospitals.

I messaged all my family to let them know the good news. They were all happy with the update. Later that evening my brother-in-law from Sweden, messaged me back to congratulate me and to let me know that the 29th of September was a special day because it was his name day and the celebration of Saint Michael. In his words, he said, "Don't worry about a thing because everything will be perfect". I was happy to hear that and I googled it to see what he was talking about.

I found that in the Catholic orthodox religious calendar, you can see that, on that day, they celebrate the three Archangels: Michael, Gabriel and, to my huge surprise, Raphael as well. I can't find the words to explain what I felt when that finding hit me.

A canvas of the Archangel Raphael was hanging on my wall. I was praying and talking to this angel every day. I had even asked him to bring me the news whenever the time was right. Not only had he done just that, but he had also given me his reassuring autograph as well. The surgery was on the day of his celebration. I cried rivers of joy and gratitude as I whispered his name again and again. How more magical could this have turned out to be?

It was like the willow tree made its appearance felt again. Its branches were dancing and swooshing a soft melody, while the sun was shining through its beautiful green branches again.

It is incredible to realise, what the power of belief can manifest. Whatever you perceive as being true to you and real, will become your experience and you will see it in your life. I believe that we send prayers to the universe all the time. Not just when we put our palms together and recite sacred words and mantras, but in every moment of our lives. The most powerful prayers are the emotions we feel, the things we repeatedly tell ourselves day in and day out, be it consciously or unconsciously, and our deepest most rooted beliefs which we hold as true.

Jesus told us the truth: All things, whatsoever you shall ask in prayer, believing you shall receive." – Matthew 21:22

To that point, I had surrendered to everything that was happening and allowed the flow to take me where I needed to be, with the faith that divine timing is the best time: not mine, but God's.

Even though I had been praying daily and waiting for that moment, I could not help having mixed feelings. I knew what was coming… theatre, anaesthesia, someone going into my head again. These thoughts had built up slowly, and one night, just a couple of days before the surgery, floods of emotions came over me and I could not help bursting into tears. It hit me that I was really close to the day when I would have to put my body under the knives again, as well as all the needles, the pain and the chemicals. Not only that, but then, there would be another recovery process, and the risk of something going wrong again.

It was very hard to go through these emotions, but I felt much better after I had cried. The biggest part of me was happy and grateful that despite the restrictions, I still had a chance to have the procedure. In addition, I knew that I was blessed beyond my expectations and that someone out there had my back big time!

THIRD TIME LUCKY

I n the morning of 28th of September 2020, one day before the surgery, my bag was packed and I was ready to embark on this journey for the third time in the last twelve months. This time around, under the pandemic restrictions, everything was very different. No friends or family were allowed at the hospital. Therefore, my sister drove me there and dropped me at the entrance that afternoon. We hugged tightly and we said goodbye.

A male nurse was expecting me. He grabbed my bag and we made our way inside, through the long hospital corridors. It felt weird to be there again. I hadn't missed it, to be honest. We had been informed beforehand that no visitors were allowed, so I knew I was going to go through it all alone this time.

That night, I could not sleep at all. I tried but it was useless. I was tossing and turning for hours. The bed seemed too small and my head was swirling with thoughts about the tall mountain I was about to begin climbing again.

In the morning, I felt like a zombie. The expert came around to check on me, and to let me know that the team was all set for the surgery. He handed me the usual protocol papers. As I read through, I could not help noticing that below the risks section, other than stroke, infection and a few other terrifying side effects, there it was again. The word we all fear. Death. I pray you never ever have to put your name on a document that includes this word. But I did; I had to.

I asked him to give my family a call and keep them updated after the procedure, and I wrote my sister's details on the back of the document. He was very kind and reassured me that he would.

After the assistant surgeon left, another team member came around to show me the metal plate that was soon going to be placed inside my head. It was so incredible and hard to grasp; I was still trying to process what was about to happen.

A few decades earlier, something like this would not have been possible. It's incredible what modern medicine can do when it comes to emergency situations. Nowadays, we are so blessed to live in a society where people have access to advanced medical care. It really saves lives.

The clock was ticking and I was feeling more anxious by the minute. It was hard not to have my family with me. My son face-timed just before I was taken downstairs; it was comforting to see his face for a few minutes.

Once again, my bed was rolling down the corridors of the hospital while they were taking me to the theatre. The feelings were still mixed. A part of me was scared, but the biggest part was excited. I kept repeating my prayers silently in my mind and that made me feel calmer.

I was happy to see the lead surgeon, Mr Bentley again. Last time I saw him was early January that year. It felt reassuring to speak to him before the surgery and I truly admired the connection and the way he was interacting with every member of his team as they were preparing and checking in for my operation. That's leadership, I thought to myself. It was remarkable and I loved feeling all that flow of positive energy just outside the theatre. I knew that I was in good hands. I went in around 8.30 am; shortly after I was put under sedatives and lost touch with what was happening.

When I regained consciousness, about six hours later, I was in the recovery room, and a nurse was calling my name. I responded with a frail voice. I'm not even sure if she heard me. I was feeling very tired. It was probably from all the chemicals, but also from the fact that I had not slept at all the night before. The previous times, I had felt a bit more alert after the anaesthetics went off, but this time I just fell back into sleep again. They kept me in the recovery room for another couple of hours, until I opened my eyes again. The protocol is to make sure you are awake and conscious when you go back to the ward. I later found out that at home, my family was beginning to worry as I was in there for too long and they didn't have any updates to that point.

They took me back to my room where I was being monitored every 15 minutes. I was sleeping most of the time. This time around, I was in a lot of pain. I remember waking up late in the evening, having an apple for dinner and asking for some painkillers. I wasn't able to masticate the food very well, so I had about half of that fruit. Still, that was a good sign.

I was also given regular intravenous antibiotics to prevent any risk of infection, due to the unfortunate history. Later in the evening, the nurse informed me that the surgeon had called my family and they were in the loop. She said that the surgery had gone very well and the experts were very happy with the result.

The next day, as I woke up, I realised that my head was wrapped in a very tight bandage. It was so hard it felt like my head was in a cast. They had warned me about this before the surgery and told me I'd have to wear it for a couple of weeks. This was to make sure that everything stayed nice and compressed so that the skin could heal well. I also had two drain tubes that were draining the excessive blood from my skull. The nurses were checking precisely how much blood was dripping in those bags. I guessed they had an expected threshold. The good thing, all was within the expectations.

I also remember finding a note that morning. It was from my nurse friend: my human guardian angel. She was working that night and she had come to see me after the surgery, but I had been asleep and she hadn't wanted to wake me up.

I was keeping my family informed via messaging, but I wasn't strong enough to talk on the phone yet. The doctors were in contact with them already and my guardian angel friend was also keeping them in the loop.

The pain was unbearable this time. The other times, my body had felt very weak, but I had not experienced that kind of pain. This time around, even though my body was feeling stronger, the pain was intense. I was taking painkillers, but that was not enough to numb the pain, and I could not get any rest at all.

Two days after the surgery, they removed the drain tubes from my head. That was the of most painful things I'd experienced in my whole life. I mean, I brought a child into this world, but I don't remember having that kind of pain. Maybe it was just a very tender phase for me, I don't know. But I literally cried when they pulled the two tubes out. It was all so painful… I just could not keep up with it anymore.

The moment they left, I drew all the curtains around my bed and cried it all out like a little baby, sighing through my tears. I had faith and I had thought I was prepared for this mentally and physically, but when it came to the real thing, it was much harder than I had imagined.

After that meltdown, it was almost like the universe felt sorry for me and gave me another miracle. The pain became more bearable, just hours after that. The next day, the third after the surgery, I got up and started to move down the corridors. I was walking very slowly but the fact that my balance was good, and I had no dizziness or other worrying symptoms made me feel so happy and confident. Gravity was on my side. By midday, I was feeling better and better and even had a video call with my family. I felt so blessed; the pain was lifted.

What I know for sure, is that all the prayers, loving energy and thoughts that I have received from my family, friends and all the wonderful souls that followed my journey is exactly what made this miracle happen. I know that whenever they thought of me or said a prayer in my name, that loving energy touched me and I was immersed in it. I say this because I felt it and it was very real.

I will forever be grateful for every soul that prayed for me that day, so if you are reading this and are one of them, I take this opportunity to thank you again and send my love to you.

My friend came to check on me again; it was lovely to see her face. We chatted for a bit and then she went out and grabbed a few things for me to eat, like fruits, juices and some healthy food products she knew I liked. That was so kind of her to look after me. It was hard to be in such situation during a pandemic, but as always, the universe has a way to send love and support when you need it most. And to me that is what she was, godsend.

The experts were checking on me regularly and were happy to see the progress. I was really glad when they said, "On Friday you can go home".

Just like that, four days went by since the surgery, and, on Friday the 2nd of October, I was sent home, with oral antibiotics and a follow up appointment to remove the bandage and the stitches ten days later.

My sister came and picked me up from the same place she had left me just days earlier. We hugged and then she carefully helped me into the car. It felt so good to see her again and to head back home together. I remember her driving with great caution as I was sitting in the backseat, nicely secured with my seatbelt on. It was a rainy day and I was enjoying the slow ride, the chat and the radio playing some nice tunes that day.

I know that for her, driving her fragile sister in the back seat, through the rain, avoiding any sudden moves and going as slowly as she possibly could, may not have been the most stress-free experience. However, once we got home, I know all her weight was lifted.

It was wonderful to be back with my family and to sleep in my own bed again. My sister was looking after me. She was cooking and juicing for me every morning to make sure that I got all the good stuff in. I was back to moving in slow motion again of course.

The first few days were very difficult, not so much for the surgery pain, as I could manage that with mild painkillers, but my head was hurting from the bandage. It was so uncomfortable to lay my head on the pillow. It felt like my head was on a brick the whole time. My right ear, which was squeezed inside the bandage, was in so much pain it was almost numb at times. I had to keep that tight until the doctor advised otherwise, to ensure that it would all heal nicely.

My teenage nephew was travelling to school every day at that time, but he had decided to move in with his dad for ten days just for my safety. When I noticed he was missing, and asked my sister where he was, I was so touched as she explained what was the situation. I remembered how thoughtful and wonderful he always is.

His intention was to keep me free of the risk of catching something, since he was travelling outside our household. He and my sister had talked about the post operation isolation, while I was in the hospital. To be honest, he didn't really have to do this. Our home was big enough and it was easy to keep my distance. I could have just stayed in my room upstairs anyway. Still, he had taken this decision on his own, as he did not want to risk it.

Even after I was better and he returned home, he wanted me to use our family bathroom all by myself, again just to be sure that I was safe until I got stronger and was out of the danger zone. What an angel.

Overall, I was managing well; at times I could not believe that I had that procedure and was already home and getting better. Time went by fast and before you know it, 45 metal stitches and the painful bandage were removed. I cannot express how much I had been looking forward to get rid of that "hat". I was ecstatic about it. I could finally get some rest and feel my head sinking into the soft pillow. I was of course still cautious and didn't sleep on my right side, until much later. Step by step, things were falling into place. It felt like I was climbing that mountain very slowly, but surely.

There was some swelling after they removed the cap and the stitches, and the inflammation was visible under the skin for a few days. However, it was amazing to see how every day that went by, the swelling was going down and my body was healing quickly. So much so, that just a week after the removal of the stitches and the bandage, the swelling was completely gone.

Every morning and evening, I would express my gratitude to the universe and thank my guardian Angel Raphael for my speedy recovery, my health and all the blessings I was so lucky to have in my life.

For many days and nights, I would fall asleep, repeating this affirmation in my mind.

"Every day in every way, I am getting better and better. I am healthier, stronger and happier than ever before."

Each morning, before I'd even open my eyes, I would repeat the same words a few times before I got up and started moving around.

I have to be honest; there were moments when I was worried that things could go wrong. On the other hand, I could not help noticing how, day by day, my body was just getting better and better. It was real and happening. The recovery happened much faster this time around, it was truly remarkable. I can't say it enough how in awe I am of the human body and its ability to heal itself. It's still a marvel to think that I have a huge piece of metal in my skull right now, and you would not even know it if I didn't tell you.

Just eight weeks after the surgery, I began to feel so good in my body that I resumed exercise. The cross-trainer was a great piece of cardio equipment to have at home; I remember setting it to the easiest level the first time I stepped on it. It was level one out of the twenty that it had, but I was happy that I could even perform 15 minutes at that slow pace.

I was looking after my body, moving and eating well, but I also paid attention to my mental and emotional health. Every day I was taking long walks in nature and enjoying the sunlight. Being in nature always helped me find that inner balance and tranquillity.

Christmas was just around the corner and my sister, my nephew and I were looking forward to spending our first one in the new home with a few close friends and family. We had such a great time decorating the house for the first time while singing along to holiday songs on the radio. Our neighbourhood was filled with Christmas lights and decorations. It felt like the whole world was looking forward to this Christmas.

Then, out of nowhere, another sudden, strict lockdown, just days before Christmas came like a brick in the forehead for everyone. The UK entered severe restrictions and I've lost count of what level of lockdown we were at the time. All I remember is having the feeling that Christmas was being taken away that year. I had been looking forward to be reunited with close family and friends, but that was not happening. The one thing that got to me the most, was the realisation that it was the first time when I would not be able to see my son for Christmas. It was a low moment, and a tough mental game for all of us. However, at least I was well, my family and friends were well, and that was something to be grateful for.

We made it through and still had a wonderful Christmas, just the three of us. The restrictions were not lifted, and we stepped into the New Year of 2021 in lockdown mode, with bubbles and a beautiful show of fireworks just above our back garden.

Weeks and months were flowing by in the New Year, and my body was feeling great and strongest than it had been in a long time. The wound was healing perfectly and, before I knew it, my hair had grown so much that it was covering it and I could not even see it anymore. My body was recovering beautifully and I was doing everything I knew to help it.

Mentally and emotionally I was in the best place I had ever been. Despite the fact that socialising in person and meeting new people wasn't much possible for any of us due to the pandemic rules; thanks to social media platforms, I was still able to connect to some pretty incredible women and human beings from UK and all over the world; from places like Bali, Sydney, and even further to Canada and USA. Being part of a strong community, interacting with like-minded souls, inspiring and supporting each other was a game changer for me throughout my healing journey. I am so grateful for all of them.

Physically I was also feeling incredible. On the cross trainer, I was now at level ten and going for 40 minutes at a time, enjoying every bit of sweat. My soul was smiling with gratitude as I remembered that, exactly one year earlier, just before the lockdown in March 2020, I had been watching the marathon under my window, longing for that feeling of nirvana from exercise and that of sweat dripping on my forehead, and now… it was real!

At that moment, I paused and asked myself, "Omg is this really happening?".

I suddenly realised that I was very close to the top of that "mountain". They say that when you climb a mountain, you should never look back, but only look at the next step in front of you.

I never climbed a real mountain before, but what I did with this mountain was to take it day by day, and step by step. At the beginning, it seemed so hard to achieve, but using this approach helped me see it through. When you focus on what's in front of you and give it your best and undivided attention, life will always reward you for it.

So, there I was, just a stone's throw from the peak, which was striking through the puffy clouds and in the background, the soul-melting blue sky. What a great feeling, what a blessing, what a miracle. I had made it to the top.

FROM MUD TO GOLD

Reflecting on a time, not long ago, when I had been on my knees, right in the middle of the biggest storm of my life, I understood that the universe had been trying to tell me something. Even though it was scary, a part of me wanted to dive deeper and understand the meaning and the lessons I had been summoned to learn. Faith had taught me that at the end of every struggle, there is always a blessing. I saw an opportunity to turn the mud into gold and I grabbed it.

This journey prompted me to ask myself major life questions. The kind of questions we rarely ever ask when the sun is shining, and the sky is blue; but only when storms are taking over our lives.

Who am I really? What is my life purpose? Who am I, without any reference to my past, achievements or future plans? What is the meaning of life? What am I supposed to learn from this?

I didn't even know where to begin. I realised that nobody at school ever teaches us how to deal with life crisis, loss or pain in life. I used to believe that my name, my status, my job and my achievements made me who I was. I thought I was a fitness coach, teaching people how to live a healthy life. I had a business, an income, and a strong healthy body. At least I had thought I did. Until the person I had thought I was, had got taken away and I wasn't sure anymore.

I had future plans, but then I hadn't been sure if I even had a future for which to plan. I had been financially independent until I wasn't anymore. I had thought I was healthy and strong until I couldn't walk on my own.

Still, I refused to define myself by the diagnosis that the doctors had given me, nor by the feeling of being a "broken doll" I had about myself at times.

I had to reconstruct myself: to redefine my true identity. Or better said… to lose the need to identify with anything external.

It's like unlearning and relearning things again. It took countless walks in nature and many diaries filled with hand-written letters: introspection, contemplation, and self-reflection, all of it, with one intention. To find these answers within myself.

I realised that nothing external could define me. Any part of me that can be taken away, cannot be part of the definition of who I am, because, when that it's gone, the sense of who I am is also gone. And so that can't be it. In fact, any definition or label we try to attach to who we are, will be diminishing, because what we are at the core, it's something that cannot be expressed or contained in any language or words.

I always knew I was a soul, in a body. We all know this intellectually. However, until you truly feel it in the depth of your heart, you never really understand it.

I dived deeper and understood that I am the awareness within my body. I realised that my body is the tool through which I exercise this awareness. I knew that the two go hand in hand. If I didn't have this body, I could only exist in spirit, which means I couldn't experience this human life. The human body and its senses are the navigating tool, but the direction is decided by this awareness.

I realised that I can have access to, and channel into this vast ocean of consciousness. No science has ever proved where thoughts are stored, but I know that when thoughts come into my mind and I become aware of what I am thinking and feeling, I have the ability to focus and choose which thoughts I want to entertain and act upon, and which to let go of. And all of this is possible because I have *free will*.

Our Creator gave us a great power. The power of choice. To exercise our awareness, and to choose. This really means that this vehicle, the human body, is equipped with the finest tools available and can create its own experiences. We can create our own trajectory, at will. Can you think of a greater gift than this?

When we go through life being unaware of this powerful gift, we may act impulsively, without recognising it. That is because, some of our decisions are driven by hidden needs and fears and we can only understand them when we take time to know and understand ourselves. We blindly grab onto worn beliefs and embody behaviours that aren't even ours to begin with.

Living this way over a long time, we lose our ability to exercise this power. We start living in our head allowing random thoughts and actions to run away with us.

In the end we disconnect from our bodies and our hearts. We stop listening to its cues and signals. We ignore it.

And then of course, life has an interesting way to grab our attention. Most of the times, it happens through unexpected events such as accidents, life crises or illnesses.

Crisis can amplify and bring more of what we hold inside, but on the other side, it can also awaken us from within. We can become more loving or we can become more bitter. It all depends on our ability to decide for ourselves.

Therefore yes, crisis will transform you, but you get to chose how.

Looking back, I can feel much has shifted in me. I am not the same person I was before this started to unfold and I am still changing every day. I guess when you come close to any death experience, your whole life perspective changes. When that shift begins to happen, you will never see things the way you used to. It alters your perception. It's as if you enter a gate that opens up into a new dimension.

One of the most valuable lessons I've learnt is that, the biggest changes in life require no physical action at all; but a great inner shift first.

To me, that was the moment life took away the paddles of my boat. Instead of resisting, which I was tempted to do at first, I had found the strength to surrender and accept it. Physically I did nothing. But inside, everything had shifted.

That is when I've learnt that letting go requires much more strength, than fighting to hold onto something. Because letting go takes a great amount of faith and acceptance, and that can only be achieved by this inner shift. By letting go of the need to fight, resist and control. By allowing life to guide you and by trusting that flow.

Have you ever watched a big bird in the sky on a windy day? I've seen that many times during my long walks in nature. I was fascinated to notice how it flaps its wings a few times and then suddenly stops and remains still with wings wide opened, completely surrendering to the strong current to keep it a float. Now that is trust! Who would have thought that surrendering can look so grandiose and calming?! It doesn't resist, complain or fight. It just allows and joins the flow. Just like the willow tree. If you look deep in nature, you will always find wisdom. Nature has been my greatest teacher.

I've learnt that despite our fears, we are built to endure anything. Our mind, heart and willingness to go on, can take us anywhere we wish to go if we trust it.

I was also reminded that I am not immortal and that life is temporary. Having to face death taught me to accept the raw truth we are all avoiding. Yes, death is an inevitable part of life. But the awareness of this truth, can only awaken us to living. I believe the biggest fear, is not that of dying, but the fear of not having lived.

I realised that no matter what I do, I can never control the moment I will be leaving this dimension. None of us can. But, I can choose to live fully while I am still alive.

This lesson helped me conquer my fears. I now know that everything flows with perfect timing. I know what is in my power and what is not. I've learnt to accept that and surrender to it in trust. Because only when you trust, you can fully surrender.

I realised that nothing outside of myself can truly fulfill me. I know it, because I had felt it. It was the moment I felt whole and perfect within myself, even though I didn't have a job, an income or any plans for the future.

That was another major inner shift. Physically I did nothing. In fact,

I was just sitting in the woods, with my back against a tree, immersed in nature. It was my "Buddha moment".

I felt worthy, completely free and happy just to be alive and simply breathing. I felt gratitude for everything in my life, from every soul I knew to every blade of grass and every breath of air my lungs were taking in. My face was filled with tears of joy. I was one with everything. It felt as if I had suddenly "crashed into serenity" and found the precious jewel of complete self-acceptance.

To be honest, I would have never thought that I'd live to see the day when I didn't feel the need to set any goals or to define a great life purpose. I never thought that I could feel worthy just because I was alive. Yet, I felt complete and absolute love and acceptance for who I am, just as I am, with no labels, and no names. What a place to be! And to reach that destination, I didn't have to do anything, or travel anywhere, but only to reach the greatest depths within myself.

I used to believe that to live with purpose meant that you have to work hard, fit into society and achieve big things. Now I know that our worth is not measured by how much we earn or what we leave behind, but by our ability to live every moment of our lives grounded in our truth, with profoundness and full presence in everything we do.

I don't think that our life purpose is confined by what we do for a living. It is my belief that *being* here *is* our life purpose; and this is directly linked to our ability and courage to make choices from a place of love and not from fear. To make choices that will free us to express our most authentic self, not choices that will imprison us. And that can only happen when our minds, bodies and hearts exist in unity and not in conflict with each other. I am convinced that with every choice we make in life, we give birth to a new reality. We change the course of our lives.

Every life we touch, interaction we have and path we cross is our purpose. A smile, a hug, an act of kindness. We make a difference just because we exist; we are more than enough, because we are a priceless element of a perfect picture. One that we can't fully comprehend through our human perception.

Many of us are blinded by status, money, beauty and power thinking that once we get that, we will feel whole and worthy.

There is absolutely nothing wrong with any of these things and we deserve it all. However, it's important that we first recognise the innate worth we already hold within. When you experience that at the soul level, none of these external things can truly enhance it. That's the place you want to be, before chasing anything else in life. That is because, when you truly know who you are at the core, you don't need anything else to complete you. You have a deep knowing that you are already whole. Your path and purpose in life becomes to live profoundly, learn, discover and express your divine beauty in human form.

And so, when you feel fully grounded in that wholeness, you are at peace with yourself. You are free. You don't need to prove yourself worthy anymore. You know that life loves you. You understand the richness of it and you value all the lessons and all the souls that touched your life, like sparkling jewels of the morning dew on a spiderweb.

I remember a close friend once asked me: "If you could go back and change what happened, would you?"

Instantly, I replied: No, I would never change a single thing, because this brought me closer to my truest self, and that, is everything.

Finally, the biggest lesson I've learnt is that sometimes pain is the only journey that can takes us back home.

THE SUNRISE BY THE RIVER OF LIFE

I hear the hum of nature just minutes before the crack of dawn. It's still dark, and I find myself sitting under the willow tree by the river. In the distance, I can hear the sweet chirping of an early bird and then another one responding, almost as an echo. I know they're speaking to each other in their own secret language.

The river flows serenely and its whispers are soothing my soul. It sounds like the loving and comforting whispers of my grandmothers and grandfathers, who are now one with Mother Nature. Everything feels so peaceful. I gently close my eyes and smile. I raise my forehead slightly as a few branches of the willow tree softly stroke my hair. I almost hear it whispering, *"You're safe my child"*. I take a deep breath in, and smile with my eyes still closed.

As the air begins to flow into my lungs, I feel like every cell of my body is soaking in some sort of love potion. What a love affair this is. The more I taste it, the drunker I get. And then I need more, and more and more.

The hum begins to get louder; more birds are chirping and joining the secret conversation. The whispers of the river seem to be rehearsing a happy song, and the branches of the willow tree are softly following the music in a gentle and almost undetectable dance.

I open my eyes, ever so gently, and through my eyelids a thread of violet light makes its way in through my senses. Oh... How beautiful this feels. Its shade changes every moment, and, as it does that, it touches my soul in ways that words cannot describe.

In the distance, I see the line between the earth and heavens. The water and the sky unite into one vast sea of light violet milk. I've never witnessed anything quite like it. The hum is getting louder and louder, the river plays the orchestra, the birds are joining in the choir, and the willow tree is dancing for this special occasion. Everything is part of this great celebration. They seem to lay this magic carpet, as if they're expecting some sort of royalty to arrive.

My eyes intuitively jump to the line between the earth and heaven one more time. And there it is, just like a king, shining at the horizon line. Ever so gentle, ever so glorious. The Sun, blessing everything that comes under its mighty light. It's a new day, a new beginning and I feel like I'm just about to dip my toes into something incredibly magnificent.

Endless Gratitude To

Ms Anna Oviedova who worked her miracles on me
Professor Keyoumars Ashkan and his team
Mr Robert Bentley and his team

And

Nicola Gammon, Eva Peña Charlón, Nicole Battwng, Mathew
Fierkas, Niki Zorzi, Niki Geddes, David Geddes, Cordelia Belgrave,
Lesley Borg, Nicoleta Kyriakoudes, Nasia Orphanides, Andreas
Andreou, Obi Nwofor, Margo Stankova, Simona Mickuviene,
Michelle Devine, Silvia Alongi, Lindsay Armitage, Sara Birkett,
Bobbie Whiteside, Hannah Sims, Jennifer Toole - Stott Young,
Dilraj Singh Virk, Dr Marios Theodotou, Dr Diamantides,
Ms Leila Stefanos Hanna and Anthony Chellappah.

If this story has touched you, pass it on.

Mari Curteanu
Mentor
www.bodysome.com

ABOUT THE AUTHOR

Mari Curteanu is the founder of BodyMind&Soul Fitness, a platform for mental, emotional and physical wellbeing. Her journey is a result of a series of bold decisions she took from a very young age. Married young, moved countries twice, changed career to follow her calling and rose above incredible life challenges. Her inspirational story is summed up in this book.

She has a background in Sport Sciences and Nutrition, combined with Life Coaching practitioner experience via the Academy of Modern Applied Psychology. Her incredible journey is a spring of daily inspiration for people around the world, and she generously shares wisdom and tools for inner transformation with her ever-growing community on her Instagram account @maricurteanu.

Her vision is to contribute to a world that is united in love, peace and harmony.

Her mission is to empower and guide people to inner transformation, self-acceptance and inner peace, and to transcend life obstacles and adversities.

Lightning Source UK Ltd.
Milton Keynes UK
UKHW040814160322
400145UK00001B/63